10⁰⁰

Figure Skating

✦ TO ✦

Fancy Skating

Figure Skating

❊ TO ❊

Fancy Skating

MEMOIRS OF THE LIFE OF

Sonja Henie

Michael Kirby

with an introduction by Scott Hamilton,
Olympic Champion and star/producer of *Stars On Ice*

Pentland Press, Inc.
www.pentlandpressusa.com

PUBLISHED BY PENTLAND PRESS, INC.
5122 Bur Oak Circle, Raleigh, North Carolina 27612
United States of America
919-782-0281

ISBN 1-57197-220-X
Library of Congress Control Number: 00-30507

Printed in the United States of America

Some dear friends who have contributed to this work with their encouragement, ideas and suggestions include: Maxine Del Prats (in London), who introduced me to Professor Edmund Boyd of Dalhouse University in Halifax, N.S., who in turn introduced me to the International Skating Union representative in Toronto, Ann Shaw.

In the past few years I have received a great deal of help in writing this book from the English professors at the College of the Desert and California State University, Coachella Valley, in Palm Desert, California. These include James Hopp, Cathy Brandt, William Gudalunas, John Norman, and especially Jack Tableshay, Joy Crites, Steve Schwartz, Wade Malthais.

Lynn Holly Johnson Givens, film star of Ice Castles and For Your Eyes Only, has made a major contribution to this book with her ideas, her facts, her syntax and structure. The author is immensely grateful.

This book is dedicated to the memory of Sonja Henie as kindly kept by the Henie-Onstad Art Center, Hovekodden, Oslo Norway, bequeathed to the people of Norway and the world by Sonja and her husband Nels Onstad, overlooking her grave and Oslo Fjord.

Table of Contents

Introduction

Michael Kirby is a man whom I have known my entire life; ours is a shared community and we certainly have much in common. Yet, after reading this book, I came to a few surprising conclusions. Though we think we know those who are close to us, in reality we can only understand a fraction of what makes them wholly who they are. Though we appreciate our loved ones, sometimes we need to take a step back to truly see their contributions of enrichment to our lives. We, each in our own way, we can touch so many of the lives that surround us without those who are affected ever realizing it. After reading this book, I realized how significant Michael Kirby is to my own life in particular and also to the world of skating.

Let me start by recounting my first exposure to Michael Kirby and his family. I remember that it was around the time when I had been introduced to skating. My parents felt that it would be important for me to witness the "next level" of competition at the Midwestern Sectional Figure Skating Championships in Troy, Ohio. The winner of the intermediate event was a young man of my age named David Kirby. I thought he was pretty cool. People were making such a big fuss over him after his gold medal win. But what really impressed me was his graciousness in accepting all the compliments flying his way. Then I noticed his family and it all made sense to me. They were so incredibly kind and supportive, and not just to their son, but to everyone present at the event. Of course, at this time I had no idea of the background of the Kirby family. Later I would discover how instrumental they were to the advancement of skating. I would come to see Michael's benign vision of skating: How it should predominately be a recreational activity for the whole family, how it can be used to instill values and promote healthy lives. (He also fostered a good time for all while lessening the often-overwhelming feeling of pressure in striving for a berth on the Olympic Team.)

Michael Kirby is a great man. His greatness is all the more heightened by the many challenges faced in his full life. As a young boy he overcame great odds in dealing with a myriad of health problems and grew to become an accomplished skater. As I previously mentioned, he is the quintessential family man. He has also been a movie star and will always be admired as a creative entrepreneur.

This is a story about a sick child that masterfully played the hand dealt to him. We follow him as a young man and see how he rises above dire financial hardship during the Great Depression to emerge successful in every way. This is a story about staying to the path and loving enough to never stray, when most would surrender. This is a story of living side by side with the legendary figure skater, Sonja Henie. This, in short, is a story of love and inspiration.

I need not go on for he shares it all in the following pages. His journey has affected everyone in skating. Now, you the reader, are fortunate enough to get a peek into a life that has been so full and so interesting. I now know so much more about this man. A man who I am lucky enough to call a friend. I hope you enjoy this wonderful book as much as I did.

See you on the ice,

Scott Hamilton

❧ *Prologue* ❧

This story is not what it is purported to be. It has the structure of an autobiography, but in order to mitigate the implied arrogance of one's own life story, it is told by the people who have really made this life what it is. So it is the story of the people who have enriched this life.

The family must of course receive first credit and importance, especially the father who was much maligned and not given the credit he deserves until too late in life. There are also the unknowns; the people in the background who could not be recognized, such as the skating judges who did so much consciously or inadvertently to further the author's career and life accomplishments.

There is one person, a woman, who had the most effect on this life without knowing that she did, and coincidentally and strangely enough, who also came into it directly in an adverse and yet contradictory, beneficial way. So this woman's effect, which was most important both directly and indirectly, makes this story her story, and in reality the biography of a world-famous woman. As will be seen, that person's effect has the influence of both good and bad, but it is always helpful, even when bad.

That person is Sonja Henie, whose fame began as a fifteen-year-old girl from Oslo, Norway. She became the youngest person to win the world championship in figure skating in 1927 and went on to win that title for ten years, as well as three Olympic titles—a record that has never been equaled. Sonja then went to Hollywood, where she was the leading box office attraction with her very popular movies. Another claim to fame came with her traveling ice show, the *Sonja Henie Hollywood Ice Revue* which was the first and grandest arena ice show in the world. She would fill such major arenas as Madison Square Garden in New York, the Chicago Stadium and other major arenas for a month at a time—an accomplishment no other skater has attained.

The purpose of this autobiography is to show, by her biography, the effect of this famous protagonist not only on the life of the author, but on the whole entertainment world. This effect was both a personal relationship and a general one which affected the author's life in every way imaginable. Since this protagonist is a famous person, her life is available in the public domain. However, the personal relationship with the author is the property solely of this author and hence is unique to him.

The author, Michael Kirby, believes that Sonja Henie is responsible for the revolution that added freestyle skating to the art and sport of figure skating. Because of her youth when she first competed in the World Figure Skating Championships (she was twelve years old), she was able to skate in a short skirt above the knee, while all the other "ladies" skated in heavy dresses down to the ankles, preventing them from raising a leg more than a few inches off the ice. Sonja copied the action of men such as Axel Poulsen, Emerich Salchow, and most importantly, the American skating prince Jackson Haines, who had first introduced the idea of doing ballet and other dance moves on ice. Sonja's mother, Selma, had seen Haines when she was a little girl and fallen in love with him and his ideas in skating. This inspired her to start Sonja in skating as soon as she could walk.

Figure skating, and more specifically free style skating used in shows (which Sonja also pioneered), created a whole new business that has provided Michael and many others with successful livelihoods, and in his case a healthy life as well as a wife and family. So Michael feels a strong debt of gratitude to Sonja. This biography is written to help display that gratitude and the creative work of Sonja Henie.

Resistance to these innovations that Sonja pioneered was felt as late as 1947 when Dick Button, the U.S. champion, was considered too "acrobatic" by the establishment in figure skating, and the championship was awarded to the person who could draw better figures on the ice. But Button was so good and the style so popular that he won the world and Olympic championships in 1948. Another concession to Sonja Henie.

The title of this book, *Figure Skating to Fancy Skating*, refers to the major transition from the sport/art of drawing figures on the ice with blades to the concept of the dance, in its many artforms, being transformed to the ice skater. Although the "American skating prince," Haines, a dance teacher, started this concept in Central Park, New York, during the late nineteenth century, it did not develop a following except in limited cities in Northern Europe. It was only Sonja Henie's talent for creative showmanship and knowledge of the dance, that created this transition in the minds of the public. Through her acumen she used the best available media at that time, the movies and newspapers, to display this new concept of figure skating. Other skaters who used this concept and built on it were Button in the 1940s, Peggy Fleming in the 1960s, Scott Hamilton in the 1980s and 1990s, and Richard Dwyer, Mr. Debonair of *Ice Follies*. Other skaters have contributed in smaller ways, because now all skaters were using and following the idea. Producers, directors, and choreographers who saw and realized its potential and made it possible for skaters to present their new ideas should also be credited with the transition. Hamilton with his *Stars on Ice*, and Button with his *Wide World of Sports* and professional championships belong in this category as well. But today the primary producers are Tom Collins with his *Tour of Champions* and agents such as Michael Rosenberg of Marco Inc., and MGI.

These individuals are really responsible for this book, as their personal encouragement and professional talent in improving and developing the concepts Sonja introduced almost a century ago. I owe them, as well as others, a tremendous debt of gratitude, such as: Arthur Wirtz, Sonja's producer and my boss for seven years; George Eby, president of *Ice Capades* and my boss for twenty years; Shipstads and Johnson, producers of *Ice Follies*; Morris Chalfen and Skee Goodheart of *Holiday on Ice* for rescuing Sonja when she was at her lowest point; Dorothy Stevens, Sonja's secretary and friend for thirty years; the Littlefield family, choreographers; Jack Pfieffer, musical director for the *Sonja Henie Hollywood Ice Revue*; Gus Lussi and Howard Nickleson, skating coaches for Sonja and others who contributed to her success; and others too numerous to name.

❖ 1 ❖

Decade One 1925-1934

"Turn left," she said to me hoarsely and timorously, although now that I think back, maybe with a touch of humor as her feminine instinct told her that the decision may have consequences other than those we both may have been aware of.

But I'm ahead of myself. This scene may really have been the start of this life, but it needs some background, so let me go back to the actual beginning and we'll get to "turn left" at the proper time.

I remember more of what my father taught me than anything my mother did, yet I was led to believe that all my parents' faults and fighting could be attributed to my father. We'll get into more of that later.

Ann McIsaac, second daughter of a prominent family of Sydney, Nova Scotia, Canada was married in April 1924 to Frederick Luke Kirby, a relative newcomer to Sydney and manager of the local Woolworth store. Ann's father, John R. McIsaac, was traffic manager for Dominion Steel and Coal Company, the largest single business in the province. As a top executive he was responsible for a fleet of freighters, colliers that brought coal from the mines of Cape Breton Island up the St. Lawrence River to Montreal for distribution to the homes and businesses of Canada. The importance of his job made him a most prominent figure in Sydney's business and social life. On a recent trip to Europe he had been booked to return on the maiden voyage of the magnificent unsinkable *Titanic*, but fortunately delays in his business caused him to miss the ship.

Ann and Fred moved into a house on a residential extension of Sydney's main business street, Charlotte Street, where their first child was born and delivered on 20 February 1925. So as not to force the prominence of her father, John R, as he was known, on her new husband, Ann suggested naming the boy after both grandfathers so he was given the name Michael John R. Kirby and was to be called Michael. He was not to be called by the popular Irish diminutive, Mike, since Ann considered that to come from a lower social level than her Scottish heritage—although it was a reflection on Fred's Irish background.

Sonja Henie: The First Intrusion

In order to simplify the progression of this narrative, we will follow it by decades and not by years, trying to pick out those things in each decade which influenced life events. To that end we can skip the first four years of Michael's life and jump to Toronto where Fred transferred as a Woolworth's manager near the main Canadian office of the company.

Shortly after the move, the young boy contracted rheumatic fever, which required a year's confinement to bed since no medication had been developed to fight this disease. For his parents to have kept a rambunctious four-year-old in bed for a year without television, or games, or even children's books must have been an act of mercy—which I hope the good Lord took into consideration when they arrived on His doorstep at relatively early ages. The boy never realized that strain his parents were under until he had four-year-olds of his own many years later.

Although his parents both died early from what we now know to be smoking connected illnesses, we have been unable to convince our own children of this danger.

The hand of fate now takes a hold of this young life. But it was a hand of fate delivered on account of Sonja Henie, her first unknown and inadvertent intrusion on this young life. Michael had barely recovered from the illness when Fred was again transferred to the Woolworth's store in downtown Winnipeg in the cold Canadian west. In looking up a local doctor to help rehabilitate the boy, his parents were going to find one who would change the entire future life of this young man! He was a general practitioner named Dr. Buck, and he had the unhappy job of informing the parents that the boy had a deformed and crippled heart valve from the rheumatic fever and would never be able to participate in normal sports. In fact, he would be frequently confined to bed or chairs for rest and inactivity and probably had life expectancy of less than forty years. His father, Fred, thought that would be a terrible life for an otherwise normal young man and asked if there was any therapy that might overcome this debilitation. This was a Winnipeg that had snow and ice for nine or ten months each year. It had a lot of ice skating since the fire department flooded every vacant lot, park, and schoolyard to form ice skating rinks. Dr. Buck said there was a new form of ice skating that was gaining in popularity. It was called fancy skating and was being popularized by a young Norwegian girl named Sonja Henie, world and Olympic champion. Dr. Buck apparently participated in figure skating, probably by following ice dancing, which involved very little athletics. He thought that it might be appropriate for the boy since he would never be able to play hockey, soccer, football, or any other contact sport. His theory was that fancy skating was rhythmical, since it was usually done to music or confined to drawing figures on the ice with one's skate blades. There was no score to meet or opponent to beat; one could skate for a few minutes or hours since it was self-regulating. Dr. Buck was probably aware of ice dancing with a partner, which was popular with older people at local skating clubs or groups, as it was not too strenuous. Neither he nor anyone else at that time could envision the extreme athleticism of the multiple revolution jumps and spins of today's figure skating. The doctor was also aware of fancy skating because it was in the process of being demonstrated by Sonja Henie who had then, in 1930, been world's and Olympic champion for four years. She had won her most recent title in New York City, where the world championships were held in 1930. It gave her great exposure in the U.S. and Canada.

Skating developed gradually over the years to the much more athletic and strenuous level it has since reached. Michael was able to follow this gradual development of skating style and develop his own muscles and heart in a way that did not put too severe a strain on it. To the young Michael this was not a serious consideration. In grammar school he went out for the track team and represented the school in the 100-yard-dash—until his parents found out and immediately took him off of the team.

Mother and Father then tried to find out all they could about this fancy skating activity and discovered there was a Winter Club in Winnipeg that included figure skating in its activities. They joined the club and found out they could take lessons in figure skating. Mother soon found out that she didn't have sufficient interest for the discipline required and did not pursue it, but Father rather liked it and participated as an ice dancer and by drawing figures on the ice. He could learn and teach young Michael.

My Viewpoint

About two years later while Dad had grown quite good at it, I had recovered enough strength. At six years old, I was to be allowed to give it a try. It cost too much to add me as a member of the Winter Club or to take lessons from the professional staff, so my father took me to outdoor ice rinks in parks and schoolyards and taught me the fundamentals of skating although none of the intricacies of figure skating yet. My first ice skates were the figure skates my mother had given up, and with the help of some thick socks, which were welcome in the frequently minus forty-degree temperatures, I learned enough about skating for my father to get me a membership in the club and begin lessons from a professional instructor.

This was a difficult decision for my family, for it was now the start of the Great Depression, and I can only imagine the strain this cost put on the family. My two sisters, Kathleen and Stephanie, had been born, and they probably were also bearing the cost to the family without realizing it. In any event I was never made aware of this hardship on the family.

I loved the freedom and self expression of figure skating, and since it was the only activity in which I could participate, I devoted as much time and effort as possible with it.

Family Activities

Another phenomenon of this first decade that was to have a significant bearing on the life of the entire family as well as myself was our summer excursions back to Sydney and our grandparents Mclsaac's house. Every summer as soon as school was out, our mother bundled us up for the train ride to Montreal, where we boarded one of the empty coal boats as the only passengers, thanks to grandfather John R, and sailed down the St. Lawrence River for four days to Sydney. What an adventure that was! It sparked my lifelong love of the sea and of boating. We had the run of the ship and were undoubtedly treated well as the family of John R.

McIsaac, the big boss! I can remember that as the ship entered Sydney harbor and we prepared to disembark, Mother would gather all the clothes we had worn for four days on the dirty coal ship and simply toss them overboard into the water. The environment was not of much concern in those days.

The visit to the house on Bayview Street was to us sheer luxury. John R always had a full stock of bananas hanging ready for us, and the kitchen was filled with every other delight we could imagine. Our uncles Ronald and John, who were still in school, seemed to take such pleasure in looking after us and taking us into town for cake and ice cream, a luxury we could not afford at home. They were all very devout, and I think I learned the value of the faith I still have from John R, as everyone including us called him, and from Ronald, John (who is still a priest), and our favorite Aunt Sarah. We felt closer to them than to our own parents and were disturbed by what was becoming an apparent big rift between our parents. Unfortunately, we children were forced to take sides in that dispute, although we didn't understand what it was all about, and Mother had the inside track on our emotions. So we were given her version of the troubles.

Later in life, second guessing my mother's motives in taking us to her home in Sydney each summer, I have decided that the latter were indeed mixed. Her parents taking the cost of feeding us for three months could justify the monetary cost of the trip. But was it fair to her marriage? Our father was left alone for three months without his family and unable to telephone because of the tremendous expense at that time; as a husband and father now I can call it cruel and unusual punishment, and for what? Obviously for the comfort and luxury of a life we could not afford—but did that in itself tell my father that he was a failure? Was it being rubbed into him that he was unable to provide such a life for us? It is a question that haunts me to this day, because that is the way in which I would have taken it. It would not have allowed my marriage to survive. In fact, just the opposite has helped our marriage survive these fifty-five years, and still climbing. It is the constant support and help I have received from my loving and wonderful wife, whether I've been a failure or success.

There was another facet to this arrangement that could also have a detrimental effect on my father. We enjoyed and loved our aunts and uncles so much in Sydney that they became our surrogate parents and family, and this must have been a further blow to my father's pride and ego.

A situation beyond my parents' control but which seriously affected their marriage was the question of birth control. After the birth of her third child, my sister Stephanie, Mother announced that she had been told that she could not, or did not want, to bear any more babies. As staunch Catholics they were not allowed to practice any artificial birth control. My father felt this to be too onerous (and I now don't blame him!) and tried to seek exception for medical reasons from the Church. Not only was he refused, but he was accused of being responsible for driving himself and his wife straight into the arms of the devil. Naturally and literally, the decision drove him from the Church and another wedge into their marriage. He began to drink more heavily, although, again from the retrospect of an experienced husband and father, it was not as heavy or as disturbing as my mother made it out to be. My father died at age fifty-four from throat cancer (from smoking we now know), and I began to realize how much I missed him—especially when I went into business and needed his wisdom and experience. All through life I have been aware of the many things he taught me, sometimes directly and sometimes inadvertently. He would listen to classical music on the radio every Sunday afternoon and get me to study or do homework in the living room with him. I am sure this gave me my liking for such music, so he gave me this interest almost by osmosis.

My like for music caused another minor family crisis. I had been given a raccoon fur coat by my aunt, as they were the latest rage on campuses everywhere. Since I was the only one in grade school with one, I disliked it, even though it helped in walking to school in forty-below-zero weather. As soon as the weather improved, I took it to a pawn shop and traded it for a clarinet—not a popular move with my family. Through the years I have realized how many ideas and attitudes my father gave me. He taught me to drive when I was about twelve years old, and I still employ his ideas in my driving. Since I have had no accidents, except one as a sixteen-year-old teen in love, and very few tickets, I think he made me a good driver.

During this decade there were few other activities that seriously affected my life; two rather trivial ones. I was taken to the dentist by Mother and told I had to have a tooth pulled. I fought this every way that I could and would not let the dentist near my mouth. Finally, the dentist called Mother out of the room for a few minutes. When they came back, the dentist prepared everything for the extraction, and as he was about to approach me, Mother suddenly jumped onto me in a straddle and held my arms immobile. There was nothing I could do, so the dentist succeeded. But it left me with a lifelong aversion for dental work from which I still suffer.

Another boyhood incident that affected my life was the time, along with some other fifth- and sixth-graders, I locked a couple of nuns into a small two-classroom extension building by piling snow in such quantities by the door that they couldn't get out! Dislike of one's teachers at that age is probably normal, but that action precipitated my move to another school run by the Christian Brothers on the other side of town. This required a very long ride on the street car, but the most uncomfortable part of this arrangement was that I had to take my lunch. For two years I had either a tomato or cheese sandwich with no butter and wafer thin slices of tomato or cheese. To this day I dislike both.

Rumors circulated that my father wanted to be transferred again, and I hoped so because I wanted to move—not only because of an aversion to the nuns and the sandwiches, but I was experiencing an unpleasant action of sexual fondling by one of the priests at the adjoining church, where I was an altar boy. It involved my first sexual experience, and it revolted me. In itself it was not too lurid, at least by today's standards, but it was quite upsetting to this twelve-or thirteen-year-old boy. The situation probably caused my lifelong antipathy toward homosexuality (please note, homosexuality, not homosexuals). My position is like the theological position—hate the sin, but love or at least, like, the sinner. If anything I felt sorry for the man, assuming that he had some kind of mental problem. This belief was confirmed a number of years later. I heard that the priest had been transferred to some institution in Toronto, where we were now living. Out of respect for the memory of his teaching and helping me in school, I arranged to meet him at the institution in downtown Toronto. The minute I was admitted to his room he turned out the lights and tried to get me physically onto his couch. I resisted and was now old enough and strong enough to prevail; but, his actions convinced me that he was suffering under some uncontrollable force that caused him to act irrationally. It certainly colored my understanding of homosexuality, which I have seen a great deal of in my later career in show business. Yet despite the past, my subsequent experience throughout my life has been most pleasant with priests and with homosexual persons. We'll get to some of them later.

Probably the most significant lifetime event of this decade was the realization that ice skating, particularly figure skating, was and would be an integral part of my life.

2

Decade Two 1935-1945

Since my marriage happened during this decade (I was nineteen), it is the most significant event of this , or any other time in my life. But a few other events led up to it and in fact contributed to it. The move to Toronto was the major factor. And Sonja Henie again inadvertently caused this major factor because she had generated increased interest in figure skating and figure skating competitions from the Olympics to the local club level.

In 1938 the Canadian National Figure Skating Championships were held at the Winnipeg Winter Club, and I qualified as a contestant in the junior division. The excitement was terrific, and the opportunity to see all the best skaters of Canada inspired me to continue despite placing fifth in a class of five contestants in the junior men! An event occurred during this competition that would have a tremendous bearing on this future life. A young girl from the Toronto area won the Junior Ladies Championship. Her name was Norah McCarthy.

In 1939 Dad was transferred back to Toronto. I was so involved with skating activities at the Winnipeg Winter Club and my skating friends that I prevailed upon my parents to allow me to remain in Winnipeg until the end of the school year—and the skating season. I was fortunate to be invited to stay with a wonderful family, the Drewrys, whose two sons were close friends and whose two daughters were tolerable.

My parents arranged for me to travel to Toronto by bus, so I chose to go via the U.S. with stops in Minneapolis and Chicago. I was fourteen and very nervous about gangsters—especially in Chicago. Each night in Minneapolis and Chicago, I took pains to hide what little money I had in every crevice or possible hiding place in the hotel room in case it was broken into. In addition to the usual door locks, I jammed a chair under the doorknob to prevent any break-in.

In Chicago I had heard of the famous Loop, and I thought that all elevated trains came into the downtown area and circled the loop before heading out on their routes. I went up into one of the stations and watched the trains for some time, until I thought I had figured out which ones were just arriving and would be circling the loop before heading out. I thought the El was exciting, and I wanted a ride on it so I could tell my friends in Canada. However, I miscalculated the train sequence and never got back to the station I started from. Instead I spent two hours going out to the end of the line, where I talked the conductor into letting me go back to the center of town without paying another fare.

Toronto

On arrival in Toronto I enrolled in St. Michael's College School near downtown Toronto and not far from the Toronto Skating Club. St. Mike's, as it was known, was staffed by priests of the Order of St. Basil, one of the best teaching orders in Canada and U.S. with schools in Detroit, Windsor, and Houston. In addition to their teaching regimen, the Basilian Fathers were extremely sports-minded; St. Mike's in Toronto was to Canada's national sport, hockey, as Notre Dame is to U.S. college football. The school was very supportive of the demands of figure skating training on my time and cooperated in every way to support my training requirements.

The family immediately became members of the Toronto Skating Club, which was a single small ice rink in a building on Dupont Street. I knew many of the members who had visited Winnipeg during the championships in 1938, so it was a most pleasant change. I had done some pair skating with a delightful young girl in Winnipeg, Margaret Chown, but we never won anything but local affairs. In Toronto I began skating with Shirley Halstead at the club, and we were lucky enough to win the Junior Pair championship of Canada in early 1940 held in Ottawa Minto Skating Club. As title holders we were invited to skate in ice show carnivals in various small towns near Toronto, including Lake Placid, which was not too far away in New York State. We were guests of the Lake Placid Club, one of the best in upstate New York. The skiing was great because it was set up for beginners like me and the slopes were gentle. Lowell Thomas, a famous commentator, taught us how to use the rope tows on the club grounds He was the Walter Cronkite of his day. After the first day of skiing, I was met in the club lobby by my partner's mother, Mrs. Halstead, who gave me a verbal lashing for being so stupid as to take a chance of breaking my leg in skiing and not being able to do the pair with her daughter, Shirley, in the ice show. Fortunately, her worries were not realized.

Sydney Again

In September 1939 Canada joined England in declaring war on Germany. As Canada went on a war footing, rationing of food and fuel began. The summer of 1940 was my last chance for a normal schoolboy's vacation free of responsibility. My father's health and condition worsened, putting a further strain on our family finances. But good old Uncle Ron McIsaac came through by offering to drive me down to Sydney with his family. He took the shortest route, which was through New York and New England, because gas rationing had not yet taken effect there as it had in Canada.

The excitement of the war became very closely related to us in Sydney. Because Sydney was the port closest to England on the North Atlantic, it was the most popular port for forming convoys for the Atlantic crossing. And my grandfather, John R. McIsaac, was at the center of that activity because of his job and experience with freighters for the Steel and Coal Company.

Another contribution to the war effort had been his personal friendship with Alexander Graham Bell, inventor of the telephone. Bell had a summer home on Cape Breton Island just a few miles from Sydney, and he and my grandfather got to know one another since they were both deaf. In fact, Bell's attempt to develop a hearing aid caused him inadvertently to invent the phone. As a result of their friendship, my grandfather had the most up-to-date telephone system, including volume control consisting of a large black metal box about eight inches square and three inches deep attached to the side of his desk. All this enabled him to become the communication center of convoy formation and control from his home. The den in his home overlooked the entire Sydney harbor so he could direct ships from his desk in this den. As a fifteen-year-old, I found this all very fascinating. I felt I was helping conduct the war. It was indeed an exciting summer and the last one I would be able to spend as a carefree schoolboy with my alter family.

The summer even had a bizarre ending. Uncle Ron could only spend a couple of weeks there, but everyone thought I could stay the whole summer, and they would find me a way back to Toronto in time for school. Well the way back turned out to be something none of us expected. Two elderly women friends of the family were driving back to Toronto as summer ended, and they offered me a ride. The first day out of Sydney on our way to Halifax to pick up the Trans-Canada Highway, the woman driving decided to try to pass a slow truck going up a hill on a two-lane road! As expected another car came over the hill from the opposite direction. The woman panicked and drove into a muddy ditch on the left side of the road. When the road became clear and she tried to drive out, she could not get traction in the mud and we were stuck! I had been driving frequently (they weren't too strict about licenses in those days), and in fact a number of my friends would deliberately slide cars into rotation on the icy roads in winter. The sides of the roads were piled about six feet high with snow banks so as we skidded into them there was no damage. So we were experienced in handling cars under those slippery conditions. After explaining to the two ladies the extent of my illegal experiences, I offered to get the car out of the ditch. Having succeeded with ease, the two women never let me get away from the driving wheel for the rest of the two thousand miles to Toronto!

I remember my father teaching me to drive at age twelve, patiently and in his usual way, thoroughly. I remember so many things about my father. I still use so many of his ideas today—the horn in the car never replaces the brake, even though you have the green light be sure to look both ways before you enter the intersection since someone may run the red light, and many more. And the trouble is that I hardly knew my father. I left home at sixteen to travel with the ice show, thinking he was a drunk who abused Mother; she brainwashed us into believing that. But we will see later she was the cause of most of his problems. Dad died of throat cancer when I was only twenty-five and working in England, so I couldn't get home for his funeral—something I have always regretted.

Canada wasn't too strict about licenses in those days, so I had had my share of driving into snow banks with my buddies, one of whom was Don Gilchrist—who had a great but inadvertent effect later on my life. We actually did it for fun. We would see who could spin the car more times before running into the snow bank! Don lived on a cul-de-sac, so there was little traffic. I figured I could spin on the ice, I was sure I could make the car spin on ice just as well. Incredibly, the deep, six-foot snow banks prevented any damage whatsoever to the car—as far as my buddies and I could see.

Other than this and a few other usual things in family and school life, this whole decade became a dedication to skating. The Toronto Skating Club was the center of skating in Canada and had more champions and potential champions than any other club in Canada. One of the highlights of my membership there was meeting a young lady named Mary Robinette. We began working on a pair routine, but I must confess that my interest was not in the sport or art of skating; I had a more personal motivation. On our first date I had to take her on the streetcar, since I did not have a driver's license yet. I was terribly embarrassed because she was a year older than I was and probably had been dated by guys who could drive. However, the next year I had my license, and the first time my parents let me use the car for a date was to take Mary to the dance following the annual carnival, which was the major skating event of the year for the club. The skating show was the predecessor of today's major professional ice shows but on a much larger scale. The orchestra was the hundred-piece Toronto Symphony so that we skated to live music. The cast consisted of all members of the families of more than a thousand members. My personal interest in Mary precluded any interest in the show or the dance afterwards, except for an incident on the way to the dance at the Royal York Hotel. As we were driving close to the hotel I realized at a stop sign that I had to make a sharp right turn. I decided to do so but discovered that there was a taxi in the way, so *smack*, I bumped into his fender. He was very nice about it and told me to go, that there wasn't enough damage to worry about. He obviously realized he was talking to a dumb young kid all dressed up for a party that he didn't want to spoil. Are there taxi drivers like that today? A different era, a different time!

The next year, 1941, I competed in the junior men's singles event at the National Championships in Montreal. In those days we skated to live music of a small band directed by the musical director of our club, in this case a great guy named Jack Jardine. Jack was our music mentor, helping us select music and interpret it for our skating numbers. There were no choreographers in those days for skating. He helped us in counting music and in such things as doing our jumps so that we reached the high point on the high note or heavy beat instead of on the landing. Many skaters and choreographers today do not realize that distinction, which makes the jump seem higher and longer. His help came in very handy later in our professional skating careers.

At the Canadian Championships in Montreal, an event (although Tonya Harding topped it with her role in the attack against Nancy Kerrigan) occurred that fit in the same mold of competitive rivalry. Just before our skating event was scheduled, Jack Jardine who was leading the live music orchestra, came up to me and said that my music had disappeared! He told me not to worry, that he knew it so well that he would play it himself from memory. At almost the same time, one of our other club members who was competing at another time in the ladies event came up to me to wish me luck and said not to worry, she had been to church that afternoon and had said a special prayer for me to do well that night. The young lady's name was Norah McCarthy, who was just another club member and friend who shared skating practice time but with whom I had no other contact or interest (that I was conscious of!). Another example of skating affecting our personal lives was Sonja Henie in action again, because Norah's interest was only caused by the popularization of skating. But I won the championship, and now I know whose prayers won it for me.

After winning the Men's Junior Championship of Canada in Montreal in February, my most meaningful award came from St. Mikes. When at the end of the school year they handed out awards for all the athletic accomplishments, I was most surprised to be given a varsity school athletic letter, the M—the first one ever given for skating other than hockey. This award was especially important to me because figure skating was considered a sissy sport by the rabid hockey fans of the school, and I had taken a good deal of good-natured kidding as being the only participant the previous two years.

Ice skating is literally the life of this decade, as it was in the previous one and will be in the subsequent ones. Dr. Buck had said that as a form of exercise it would gradually develop the heart and help it overcome the deficiency of the weakened heart valve; he seemed to be correct, since I was having no weakness in physical development and was gradually developing physical strength as the requirements of skating grew more rigorous. In Dr. Buck's days, men did not lift their skating partners over their heads, yet I was now able to do that constantly. In fact, when I was a member of the fours, a group of two partners skating together as a group, my partner was Marie Therese (Tasie) McCarthy, sister of Norah. I took weightlifting exercises at the YMCA in order to help me lift the girls.

In the fall of 1941 I began to train for the National Men's Championship, since as Junior Champion I could not repeat in that division. My father was having serious physical and mental problems, which led to serious financial problems for the family, but they were still able to help me continue training albeit at a much reduced expense. I was lucky to get one skating lesson per week from our coach (at one dollar each!), but the atmosphere of the club and the camaraderie of the skaters helping one another gave me the encouragement and assistance I needed. After skating an exhibition on a Saturday afternoon ice dance session—which the club offered to give the competitors some experience—I was approached by a Mr. McCreath, the father of a man who had been the Canadian champion but was then in the service, since Canada had gone to war with Germany. McCreath told me that I was terribly out of condition and should do exercises to improve my conditioning. He proposed that I run to the club every morning when I came to practice my skating figures before going to school. I don't remember how far it was, but I do remember that I was so tired when I got to the club that I could not skate and just crashed on the hard wooden benches in the locker room. It occurred to me that maybe he was expecting his son back from the war, so he was trying to get me out of the way! It did begin to help me, however, and my conditioning improved accordingly, so I realized how foolish my negative thoughts were about McCreath—although Ralph came home when the war was over in 1945 and won the championship in 1946.

The Canadian Championships of 1942 were held in my old hometown of Winnipeg in January. The senior men's division had only two competitors, Don Gilchrist who had been runner up to McCreath for many years, and myself. Those who know the difficulty and complexity of today's figure skating standards with their triple and quadruple jumps will be amused to know that the most difficult jumps in my championship program in 1942 were two of the now simplest double jumps, the salchow and double loop. In my championship attempt I missed the salchow but still earned enough points to win the Men's Championship of Canada! Don's mother confronted me in the club lobby after the results were announced and said, "Michael, how could you? This was Donny's year."

Over the years Don and I became good friends, and he was able to get even many years later in a unique and humorous way. Don was attending the London School of Economics for postgraduate work in 1950 and 1951 while I was skating in the musical play, *Rose Marie on Ice*, also in London. Don frequently attended the show with his movie camera shooting different parts of our routines. One night when he was filming one of my solo numbers, I took an inglorious pratfall while trying to do my normally easy single axel jump. Of course Don had this on film. Years later, when he was Consul General of Canada for Los Angeles each year he would have a reception for all the champion skaters who appeared in Tom *Collins' Tour of Champions*. During this party Don would get out his voluminous library of amateur films including the one with my fall during *Rose Marie on Ice* in London. That was bad enough, but just to rub it in he would rewind and play the fall over and over again, to the intense amusement of all the world's famous skaters and my intense chagrin!

Don remained in amateur skating and became an international judge and official in charge of many international skating competitions. Sometimes I wonder if that kind of dedication to the advancement of the sport is a greater contribution than our professional show skating was. For a few years while we were living in Newport Beach, he was Canadian Consul General in Los Angeles so in addition to skating events we saw a good deal of each other's families.

At the end of that school year I was again awarded a varsity letter, and I treasured it as much as the first one. During that school year I became involved in the acting group and the debating society, both of which would make substantial contributions to my future career opportunities, as we shall see—and all thanks to the help and encouragement of my English professor, Father Norbert Clemens of the Order of St. Basil. This mention reminds me that we heard of the bombing of Pearl Harbor by the Japanese navy while we were rehearsing a play in the school theater in the afternoon of 7 December 1941, "A date that will live in infamy," as President Roosevelt put it.

Father Clemens was not only helpful in the acting and debating exercises but in many informal discussions on philosophy, theology, and other historic and religious subjects.

At this point in my career, somehow I acquired the nickname "Cas." However my friends' reasons were unfounded. In my search for the best partner, I innocently skated with a number of different girls. My friends felt, therefore, I earned the dubious distinction of being a Casanova. It may have looked lascivious at the time, but little did they know I would eventually end up with the two best partners I could ever ask for: one for life and one for a career.

❧ 3 ❧

Turning Pro

Although I strongly dislike and disagree with both words in this title, I use it because it is the common vernacular. The word "turning" is usually associated with a traitor, and I think that was the original connotation of using it in reference to someone for leaving the hallowed pristine ranks of amateurism in the days of class distinction of patronism to become a traitor to the blandishments of the lowly pieces of money. And I have always contended that the word "pro" is an adjective and not a noun. An amusing incident occurred on the subject of the word in Houston a number of years later when George Eby and I attended the opening of our new Chalet at the Houston Galleria. We attended a restaurant in the hotel, and it was very crowded, so we asked the waitress if it was always this busy. She said, "Yes, and sometimes even busier. You should have been here last week when the such and such convention was here. Every pro in town was working this place." You can imagine what noun that word "pro" modified. But back to the present.

The championship title helped considerably later that year when it was apparent that I had to go to work to help the family. The offer from a major ice show was considerably more than I could have earned locally. To give you some idea of the perspective, I was able to earn eighteen dollars per six-day week the previous summer in a local plastics factory. My father had lined up the job for me because he knew I was interested in the future of plastics, even though the only things made of plastic in those days were combs and toothbrush handles. I had also worked for a few weeks at the Aunt Jemima pancake booth at the Canadian National Exposition in Toronto flipping pancakes for ten dollars a week. But the *Ice Follies* offered me seventy-five dollars a week to start, with the assurance that it would go to $125 per week as soon as they could find a specialty number for me. So I rationalized that I would make a fortune in a couple of years and then come back to college and get into the plastic business. But now we were under threat of eviction for nonpayment of rent. The landlord would not accept the word of a sixteen-year-old that I would clear up the rent delinquency from future earnings, so I turned to my uncle, Ron McIsaac, who was now an executive with the Woolworth Company's main office in Toronto. Ron gave me postdated checks to cover the rent, and I covered them with my own postdated checks, even though I had yet to earn my first paycheck. Thank heaven Uncle Ron trusted me.

I was the national champion, best in all of Canada. Now it was finally my turn to really give back to the family. When you're eighteen years old and you tell your family you've made a plan for the rest of your life, what are the chances that everything falls in place just as you planned? A fortune in two years of show skating, college, and then the plastics business. My plan worked precisely. I found myself in the Hollywood business, where there were more people made of plastic than you could count in a Mattel factory. There were definitely a few two-year periods where I made a fortune and was equally adept at spending (misplacing) it. And indeed I did enter college, half a century later. Well my family may not have been there every step of the way, but God was definitely my copilot, which is why I still have faith.

There was a further complication. Canadian law prohibited males of army age to leave the country without an "Exit Permit" from the national government in Ottawa. Again, the family came to the rescue in the form of my uncle Fabe Poulin, husband of my mother's older sister, Mary. Uncle Fabe had many connections in the federal government and was able to expedite the exit permit because I had already been turned down by the Canadian draft. So I was able to leave the family after Christmas and join the *Ice Follies* for their playing date in Philadelphia.

What happened and why do I still have so much faith in God's help in our lives? A few months after I joined the show in Philadelphia in January 1943, one of the principal male skaters was called in the U.S. military draft. I was asked to form a pair number to take his place. I had been drafted in Canada, since it had declared war, but was turned down because of my heart condition. After joining *Ice Follies* and becoming an official resident with a green card, I was also called up by the U.S. draft but again was turned down for medical reasons. Little did I know that serendipity was beginning to knock at my back door. Serendipity by the name of Sonja Henie. When the producers needed to replace the draftee who was skating a lead pair, they asked me to prepare a pair number. This was in the ice show, *Ice Follies*, which grew out of the *International Ice Revue*, which Sonja Henie had started in Chicago in 1936. Could the influence of Sonja Henie be any more in evidence? And who should the show decide that I would skate with but Norah McCarthy!

So Norah and I made up the pair routine to finish up that year's tour, and during the summer while the show played in San Francisco, we prepared new numbers for the new edition of the show—which was scheduled for a major Hollywood premiere in Los Angeles in September. Within the year of our joining *Ice Follies*, my two sisters, Kay and Stephanie, and Norah's sister, Tasie, also joined the show when they finished high school. It was much more interesting and fun than working at home in a factory or office. In my sisters' case it also gave them a chance to move away from an unpleasant home. The growing rift between Mother and Dad would not let me answer their call.

Opening night in Hollywood was the major event of the year. The Pan-Pacific Auditorium would be filled to capacity, with dozens of Hollywood's biggest stars filling the best of the best seats. The glamour and glow of Hollywood was so grand, and now we were actually a part of it. It was on this night that the world changed. And it all began with those two words: "Turn Left!"

On the premier night in Hollywood, it was customary for the stars of the show to go out on the ice during the intermission to greet the many Hollywood film stars who were in the audience and have pictures taken for publicity purposes. One star in attendance was Edgar Bergen, a world-famous ventriloquist with a very popular weekly radio show in which his star dummy was Charlie McCarthy. Some photographer or public relations person had the idea that since the star of *Ice Follies*, Norah McCarthy, had the same name as Bergen's dummy, it would be clever to photograph Norah on Bergen's knee as a replacement for Charlie. The intermission, however, was coming to an end, and Norah had to go backstage and prepare for her skating numbers in the second half. They made arrangements for Bergen and Norah to meet after the show and do the photo. Those of us in the cast had planned a celebration party back at our hotel after the show so Norah and I were disappointed that we had to stay at the arena, but we knew the publicity was important, so I agreed to wait for Norah and drive her back to the party. We were driving north on La Brea Street when I mentioned to Norah that someone had told me that on a beautiful night like that night, the moon on the surf at the beach was so bright that it caused the phosphorous in the water to glow like fireworks. As we approached Sunset Boulevard I told Norah that if we were to go to the party we had to turn right to the hotel; or, if we wanted to see the moonlight on the surf, we should turn left toward the beach. To my astonishment, she said, "Turn left."

But fate would play a hand in our lives again. As we got about halfway to the beach, in Beverly Hills we were suddenly engulfed in fog so thick I could hardly see the front of the car. We decided there was no point in continuing since the fog would block any moonlight from shining on the water, so we decided to turn back to the party. The thick fog on a busy Sunset Boulevard prevented me from making a U-turn, so I turned right onto a side street in order to find a safe place to turn around. To our surprise we were in Bel Air, and the road kept climbing up the hill with no easy place to turn since all the driveways were gated and the road was too winding and narrow. Suddenly we were above the fog. The hill we were on was like an island rising out of the sea, and other hilltops nearby resembled the rest of our own archipelago. I saw a vacant lot I could turn into and park. It was so magical. I put the top down on the rented convertible so we could finally enjoy the moonlight we had set out for.

Like an ascending jet when it breaks through the turbulent clouds, all of a sudden there is a clarity, a floating peacefulness when you realize you've left all the madness behind. And perhaps all that matters is the one beside you. For a time nature's beauty created a silence so palpable one could cleave it with a knife. But my curiosity eventually trounced on my apprehension. I asked Norah if she had a date that night since she seemed to have a date in every previous town we had played. She said no, but that a friend from San Francisco might come down to Hollywood. I said I was surprised that she did not have a date because it had amused me to see all these guys date her for a while, then seem to "fall by the wayside and disappear." Norah warmly replied, "Except you."

I felt a chill run up my spine, and I still do today when I recall that moment. I feebly said, "But I've never been a date of yours."

"I know that, why not?"

All of her dates had seemed older, more mature and sophisticated than I was, so I stood on my pride and admitted, "I didn't feel I could run in that field."

"Why not? You're leading it."

It's amazing the honesty the right ambiance can bring forth. And incredibly fate had created it. To just fall upon a moonlit hilltop? Our own majestic island? Neither one of us sought this place. She had softly, timorously said, "Turn left," and now my heart was turned upside down. They say love will find you and as much as I wanted to believe that I instead chose to convince myself that I was merely in the game. Norah had only given me an opportunity. I would still be competing with the real heavyweights. But at least I was in the game!

As we drove down the hill and back into the real world, we were once again engulfed in the fog along Sunset Boulevard. Naturally, I drove very carefully. Strangely enough, it was so thick that I could not even see the front of the car. But I could not dare be intimidated now in front of Norah. She had put me in the game for heaven's sake, first string. And besides my driving experience had been abundant, and I had driven in a variety of weather patterns. So I simply drove by following the yellow center line from my side window. Suddenly the lights of a police car were right behind me! The officer asked what I was doing. I told him I was being extra careful because of the fog. He said, "What fog?" and had me step out of the car. It was a beautiful, clear, moonlit night! Apparently, while we had been in a fog, literally and figuratively, we collected so much condensation on the windshield that I could not tell when the fog had dissipated. Surely there was no other natural phenomenon that could have clouded the windows. Right?

❧ 4 ❧

Movie Contract

The next morning I had a call from a Ned Dobson, who introduced himself as an agent with the William Morris agency, one of the biggest in Hollywood. He told me that the casting director of Metro-Goldwyn-Mayer Studios (MGM) had seen the ice show the night before and wanted to meet me and discuss an acting contract! I jumped at the opportunity to meet with Billy Grady, head of casting for the studio.

At the meeting in his office at MGM, I told him that except for being in a couple of plays during high school, I had never really acted and could not be considered an "actor." Regardless of having now properly shot myself in the foot, he advised that they were not interested in me as an actor but simply as a "personality." They wanted to do a screen test to see if that personality came through the camera.

It's an odd thing to be told someone is going to test your personality to see if the camera can detect that you have some. It is sort of like a first date—you hope the gal fancies your personality. But yet with a camera, that's so mechanical. Can you hope the camera uses the right lens, the best personality detection lens? And what happens if I fail? I go through life realizing that a piece of machinery has failed to pick up an inkling of personality. Would I tell Norah the results? She'd probably take me out of the game. I'd be benched right at the top of the season.

Grady made arrangements for the test, during which I was assured, once again, I wouldn't have to act but just be myself while he stood beside the camera and asked questions. Be myself! I'm being tested on being me. How do I study for this? What if I don't have the right answers? By then I wished my first response was, "Actually I'm a highly trained actor. Ice skating is just a gig I picked up in between jobs. Thought it'd be fun, so may I do a monologue for you, something from perhaps Hitchcock's latest thriller, *The Mulholland Fog*?"

A couple of days after the screen test, Grady called and asked if I would like to bring any family member or friend to see the test with me. My family were all back in Canada, and besides they already had eighteen years of being tested by my personality. Having abided by the rules Mr. Robinette set, who had made me promise not to date Mary which probably contributed to my love with Norah. Mary and I had not dated or even hardly spoken. Perhaps her father had already used that personality detection lens and had now achieved his desired result. The person who constantly appeared in my mind as the one I would like to watch and comment on the test, and be honest with me about it, would be Norah. So, throwing caution to the wind, I asked her, and she agreed to come with me.

After we viewed the screen test, we returned to Mr. Grady's office, where he informed me that MGM liked the test and wanted to sign me to a contract as an actor. This was flattering and exciting, but I had just agreed to a new contract with *Ice Follies* because Norah and I had a prominent role in the new show. I told Mr. Grady that although his offer was more than double what I was making in the ice show, I felt obligated to honor my contract with *Ice Follies*. Clearly, my plan of making enough money to go to school and then work in the plastics factory was not on the tip of my tongue. I'm sure, subconsciously, I didn't want to be separated from Norah when things looked so promising. I countered with the offer to start a new contract with MGM in one year when the skating tour ended. He thought that would be agreeable to MGM. A contract was written up with a start date of September 1944.

I also wanted it in writing that they were hiring me as more than just a skater. I was well aware that although Sonja Henie movies had been popular, they were beginning to fade, and there seemed to be very limited appeal or show business interest in ice skating. So to allay this concern they agreed, and a phrase was added to the contract to the effect that they were not hiring me solely as a skater, and that they would train me to be an actor.

With that settled, Norah and I resumed our work for *Ice Follies* and began the year's tour to see if we were just pair skating partners or maybe something more. As the tour went on, city after city, we worked more and more closely, both on and off the ice. The whole year took on a much stronger dimension as we realized that we were perhaps falling in love.

There were many bumps along the way, and I don't mean bumps on the ice, although there were a few of those too. Norah's boyfriends from previous visits to their towns showed up with high hopes of renewing their friendship, and occasionally Norah accepted, "just to be sure her true feelings were in the right place." But that didn't pacify me very much.

The show played Philadelphia for a month starting at Christmas, so many of the skaters took apartments to avoid hotel expense. Norah and her sister Tasie roomed with a couple of other girls in the show. They decided to have an old-fashioned, family-type dinner and invited a number of other friends from the show. With so many people coming, she bought the biggest turkey she could find only to discover we had to hammer the pot down to fit into the tiny oven. Norah was not sure of how long it took to cook a turkey since this was her first, but after a little while it looked terrific, so we took it out and started carving. Well, it was raw! Our "old-fashioned" Christmas dinner consisted of vegetables. We could have become the first vegans. However, I must add quickly that Norah soon became an excellent cook and still likes to experiment with new dishes, all of which are interesting and delicious. Gratefully, vegetables have maintained their title of side dishes.

The worst experience for us during that tour year happened in Boston on opening night. We arrived in town in the morning and went to the Boston Arena, which was in the same building as the hotel, for a workout to prepare for the opening. During the practice Norah felt her skates weren't sharp enough for the hard ice there. Hockey players liked very hard, cold ice, and the members of the Boston hockey team were so popular that they got what they wanted. The man who usually sharpened our skates was not around, or else I just wanted to show off and impress Norah, so I sharpened her skates. But I did a terrible job! As our number was the first one in the show, there was no time to try them out. It was a lavish, formal ballet number with simulated ostrich feather trees surrounded by satin settees. We began our number with entrances from opposite sides of the stage, and as we came together to meet in center ice, I could see a look of panic on Norah's face. She wasn't able to stop and we sort of crashed together! She told me she couldn't control her skates. They kept sliding sideways and would not bite into the ice. We were able to do the parts of the number when we were together, but whenever we parted she could not glide properly or stop, so each time we separated she fell. It happened so often that our sisters and others in the chorus watching us from the settees started to cry. But then at the end of the number in our final move, which was to give it a dramatic ending, I fell down and slid under the huge hoop skirt of one of the chorus girls.

Well at that point the audience thought that our number must be a comedy, and they started to laugh. That's when it really hurt. Roy Shipstad, one of the owners, was watching and knew what was wrong. He ran backstage to look at Norah's skates. Instead of sharpening the edge of the blade that must cut into the ice to prevent it from sliding uncontrollably sideways, I had taken one of the edges completely off the blade so it was like skating on a coat hanger. Roy was able to fix them so she could skate her solo number properly. This was in front of a full house of sixteen thousand people, because it was a special war bond benefit performance. People who bought a certain amount of war bonds received free tickets to *Ice Follies* for that night. And since opening night is covered by the local critics, we were prominently reported for our questionable performance. Having been the cause of that embarrassment for Norah, it is surprising that she ever spoke to me again let alone married me!

Closing night performances are always filled with hi-jinx, even though "the boys," as the Shipstads and Johnson are known, warned us against this, but it happens anyway. At the end of our skating number Norah and I as the Caliph and his bride, moved to a throne while others came out and performed in our "court." Two of these performers were brothers who did a pair routine. As part of their entrance they skated up to our throne and presented us with gold boxes of gifts. On this last night as they bowed in front of us, and then they each opened the boxes, shielded from the audience, took out water pistols, and sprayed me right in the face. I couldn't recoil or duck or I would ruin the scene, so I had to sit still and take the full shot of water. They were the Galbraith brothers, and one of them, Sheldon, became a famous skating coach in Canada with many champions, including the world and Olympic champion, Barbara Ann Scott.

As we did after so many shows before this night, we took our bows and the curtain fell. But this night was different. Norah and

I would be separated for one month, and we both had mixed feelings about leaving Minneapolis. Our days together so far had been planned and organized—no questions to ask, no time to meander or wonder. Such is life on the road, seven or eight shows a week. But now for one month each of us would contend with opportunity knocking at our doors on a daily basis for other interests. I felt confident, but part of me hoped this vacation would not be a test for Norah and me. Our reluctance to take this step and lengthy good-byes caused us to miss our train to Chicago. As I recall we were quite busy. But home was calling, and I eventually made it to Toronto while Norah went on to North Bay.

During our month-long spring vacation, both Norah and I told our parents that we were thinking of the possibility of getting married. My parents thought Norah was wonderful and would be great help for me, but Norah's mother thought, like all girls' mothers, that no man was good enough for her daughter. Blanche McCarthy even used the argument that I was scheduled to die at forty and Norah would be left a forty-year-old widow. I wish Mother McCarthy had stayed around long enough for me to prove her wrong.

After the vacation we convened in Minneapolis to take the show train out to our next play date, Seattle. On the second evening shortly after we left Spokane, the monotonous drone of the train wheels crescendoed to a thunderous clap. I was tossed around the cubicle washroom to a score of echoing cymbals as I realized the train jumped the tracks, turned over, and slid down an embankment on its side. I heard gurgling and water flowing like a mountain stream in spring and immediately recalled the river we had been traveling along side for the past few hours. Burial at sea had always been my plan, but not this way. I was afraid we were sliding right into that river. I fought my way out of the cubicle and climbed the floor, which was now the side wall, in order to make my way to the end of the car and freedom. I was relieved to see the wise old river had veered away from our "mis-tracks" just minutes earlier. Flying glass and cutlery cut and bruised passengers in the dining car. Our car settled at the bottom of the embankment, so I climbed back in to retrieve my first aid kit. As I pulled my suitcase from under my seat, an army officer who was a passenger pulled his sidearm out and pointed it at me. "We shoot looters," he stated callously. The gun looked like a cannon to me, but I was able to convince him that I was trying to be helpful. Like a hunter who's best shot was startled and ran, he put the pistol away, and I breathed again.

After a couple of weeks in Seattle, we went on to Portland, Oregon. While there we heard the announcement of D-Day in Europe, and the town exploded! People were singing and dancing in the streets with excitement. The confidence of impending victory overcame the realization that our soldiers and sailors were dying over there for us. I learned later that Dwight Eisenhower, Supreme Allied Commander, had actually prepared two announcements before the invasion. One proclaimed the success of the landings, but the other announced that our troops had to withdraw in the face of overwhelming resistance, which showed the fragility and risk of this enterprise.

After Portland we moved to San Francisco, where the current edition of the show played every night and we rehearsed numbers for the new show, *Ice Follies of 1945*, which would open in Hollywood in September. Just as before, the cast dispersed to various apartments throughout the city. Norah and her friends took an apartment in the Pacific Ocean section, and a few of my friends took an apartment on the fifteenth floor of the Clay-Jones building on Nob Hill. We could look down into the Top of the Mark room of the Mark Hopkins Hotel a couple of blocks away. I'll never forget that for a variety of reasons.

Since we played in San Francisco for about three months each year, we made a number of close friends. One who was a great friend and supporter of the show was Frank Schwabacker, a young banker who helped a number of skaters with their banking needs. He would come almost every night and sit in the same front row seat, cheerfully returning our acknowledgment to him during our numbers.

The other cast members spent their days rehearsing next season's new show, but for me, September and my new contract with MGM was not far off. This freed up my days to visit San Francisco friends and also give my best effort at being the chief cook for my roommates who did have to work every day. My cooking skills were nonexistent, but with many calls to Norah I came up with a few culinary miracles. Among them was cooked beets that still resembled beets, complete with their crimson tincture. With Norah guiding me through each meal, by phone, none of my roommates starved that summer. And the renowned

Culinary Institute of San Francisco lost a potential valedictorian to MGM Studios.

As the summer wore on, Norah and I knew that we wanted to get married. My reasons were obvious, with Norah's wonderful personality and beauty, but I had a deeper reason; I felt that Norah would help me get to heaven! Sounds kind of altruistic and holier than hell, but I meant it and still do. Another reason may have been my desire to have my own family and do better with it than I felt my parents had done with their marriage and family. My youth had not been spent in the happiest of family environments. I felt Norah and I could improve on that.

My contract with MGM had annual increases scheduled every year. I felt I could support a wife and the children we wanted. Of course each year was subject to an option, but I did not know what an option was and left it at that. Billy Grady and the big boss, Louis B. Mayer, whom I had met with Grady, were so positive about me that now even I was confident I could be successful in pictures.

During the summer in San Francisco we met Father Tom Reardon, who was on medical leave as a chaplain in the U.S. Navy. He had contracted malaria during the horrible battles for Guadalcanal and was prominently mentioned in Richard Tregaskis's famous story about that fight, *Guadalcanal Diary*. We wanted him to marry us in October, but he had some doubt as to how long his leave would be due to the continuing fighting in the Pacific, where he had been stationed.

Then there was *Ice Follies*. Norah had become such a popular star during the previous tour with the show that they begged us to put off the wedding. Norah made it clear that when she married she would leave the show and stay with me. But Father Tom had gotten word that he would not have to report back until right after Christmas, so we reached a compromise with the show. Norah would remain with the show until December, which would cover their three main cities—Los Angeles, Chicago, and New York. Closing night in New York in mid-December gave Norah the perfect opportunity to visit with her family in Canada and then come out to California on the Super-Chief. This pushed the wedding date back to 23 December, which spoiled a few Christmases over the years but enhanced just as many holiday seasons too.

Schwabacker's front-row charisma led him to know all the right people, including a good jeweler. I bought the best engagement ring money could buy. Well, my money anyway. It took all the savings I had, but my banker assured me my portfolio would remain intact! Right after the show we threw a birthday party for Norah on 25 August at the Top of the Mark. During the party I was able to coax Norah back to her apartment, where I had hidden the ring. Once there I went down on my knees, presented her with the ring and formally asked her to marry me. She didn't even hesitate. With her emphatic yes reverberating in my heart we rushed back to the party at the Mark to share the news, where Norah's newly adorned hand was rivaled only by the sparkle of her smile. I watched Norah as she seemed to float through the room and was reminded of the foggy night when my skating partner told me to turn left. Now I knew in my heart this was really right. And Casanova could never have caught a gal as classy as Norah.

My new career at MGM was far from what had become the well-trodden choreography of life on the road, ice-show life. The studio kept me busy with drama class, speech lessons, and interviews for roles in movies. Still, I had a lot of time on my hands. There was an ice rink in Westwood Village, called the Sonja Henie Westwood Ice Palace, near where I had a room at a rooming house. I spent a good deal of time there trying to keep my skating in condition. This was another subliminal occasion of Sonja Henie coming into my life. In fact, the Sonja Henie Westwood Ice Palace would be the vehicle that took me to my personal meeting with Sonja. No matter how far this new career was going to take me, I knew I shouldn't let go of my one solid strength. Physically and mentally, I couldn't afford to lose skating. My championship titles were my calling card, and without solicitation numerous people requested lessons from me. For the first time I began to teach. The requests were so frequent that rink management gave me permission to teach independently. Among my pupils were Shirley Temple; Cyd Charisse's daughter; Richard Dwyer, who became star of *Ice Follies* as "Mr. Debonair"; and Ronnie Robertson, whom, "believe it or not," Robert Ripley called The Human Top, and an international competitor before becoming the star of *Ice Capades*.

It wasn't long before I began work on my first picture. *Keep Your Powder Dry* was a film about the new women's army. I played an army officer just married to a woman who had joined Woman's Army Corps (WAC), and we were on a short honeymoon before both of us had to return to duty. The scene was in our hotel room, and we were both costumed in dressing gowns. In those days that meant both of us were sealed up from floor to neck like Jacques Cousteau on a deep-sea safari. When my mother saw the film she thought it was risqué and conjured in her mind that Hollywood had already gotten to me! My "wife" in the picture was a lovely young star named Susan Peters. As soon as we finished the picture she went back East and looked up Norah in the ice show to tell her that I had not "gone Hollywood" and was anxiously awaiting her arrival. Shortly after filming, Susan was in a horrible hunting accident with her husband. She was paralyzed and confined to a wheelchair, which ultimately ended her career. She was a lovely leading lady.

As a film was being edited there was a process called looping going on simultaneously. If an actor said a line incorrectly, or if ambient sound muffled the line, or even if the director felt the line should resonate a different feeling, the line could be "looped" or rerecorded. The scene with the line to correct was spliced on to a continuous circle or "loop," which was played over and over again. The actor watched the scene, and each time it came around make his best attempt at visually synching the new line. I was in the projection studio preparing to do my loop when Lana Turner, the star of the film, rushed in and asked if she could go first—she had another important date. I of course said yes and started to leave, but she said I should stay since she only had one line to do.

They played the line for her, and she really laughed at it. It was a scene in her lavish Park Avenue apartment bedroom. Her maid comes in and wakes her, saying that her lawyer is there to see her on some important matter. Lana, in bed, rolls over, covering her head with the sheet, and says, "Tell him to sue himself." She laughed, turned to me—the only other person in the room—and said, "That sure sounds like I told him to go screw himself, doesn't it?" Well I had honestly never heard a girl or woman use such a dirty word and to say the least I was truly shocked. But this was Hollywood, and I figured I was about to be shocked more than once.

A new film was opening, and the studio publicity department said I was to take another young contract player, Frances Rafferty, to the premiere. Being a true gentleman I vowed, "I can't do that, I'm engaged to be married next month."

They declared, "That doesn't matter, this is business, and the studio wants you both to get publicity. And besides, it's in your contract." I obliged, feeling very uncomfortable but realizing it wasn't the most unlawful thing after all. Frances was fun and in the same boat, she was going to get married shortly thereafter. She was a bit flippant and claimed she would wear padlocked red flannel underwear on her wedding night. I've always remembered her for that. Today I wonder, if I was so uncomfortable, how did we get on that subject?

Frances was one of many "contract players" in the studio. We got to know each other very well since we were all at the same stage of our training. Some went on to success and some disappeared. We all shared a corner of the commissary at MGM for lunch with other beginning musicians such as Stanley Donen, an assistant dance director who became a director of such greats as *Singin' in the Rain* and *Funny Face*; Andrè Previn, a young pianist whose talents shot him to the top as a world famous conductor and composer and who was then Mia Farrow's husband. The actors included Piper Laurie, Marjorie Lord, Tony Curtis, Cameron Mitchell, Marshall Thompson, Jon Archer, Marie Windsor, and many others.

Flying over the Alps at St. Moritz

Sonja and the King of Norway

Sonja in front of her home in Oslo

Sonja as youngest competitor in World Championship circa 1928

Before introducing white boots

Her famous Hawaiian hula on ice

Universal - International
PRESENTS

SONJA HENIE
in
the COUNTESS of MONTE CRISTO

SONJA HENIE

PRODUCED BY
John Beck

DIRECTED BY
Frederick
De Cordova

MICHAEL KIRBY

'The Songs'

"WHO BELIEVES IN
SANTA CLAUS"

"THE FRIENDLY
POLKA"

OLGA SAN JUAN

WHO BELIEVES IN SANTA CLAUS?
(From the Universal-International picture
"The Countess of Monte Cristo")
Jack Brooks   Saul Chaplin

Who believes in Santa Claus?
I do! Do you?
I believe there's a guy with
A twinkle in his eye,
Who can fly thru a sky of blue.
Who believes in Santa Claus?
I do! Do you?
I believe when you're good
You get ev'rything you should,
And I'll tell you why I do.
Who makes the children happy
At this time ev'ry year?
Why it's old Saint Nick
With a candy stick and a bag of
    Christmas cheer.
Who believes in story books?
I do! Do you?
When you believe ev'ry word,
Ev'ry story that you've heard
Is honest to goodness true,
You'll believe in Santa Claus too.
Copyright 1948 Robert Music Corp.

with
Olga San Juan

Dorothy Hart

Michael Kirby

Arthur Treacher

Hugh French

Ransom Sherman

Freddie Trenkler

. . . .

THE FRIENDLY POLKA
(From the Universal-International picture
"The Countess of Monte Cristo")
Jack Brooks   Saul Chaplin

When work is done,
It's fun to get away and spend
A friendly night, with the folks
Whose jokes you've heard
A hundred times, but
Still you laugh with delight.
And when you toast your host
Be sure you don't forget the ones
Who can't be here.
So drink to your friends,
And friends of your friends,
And don't forget your Uncle Ola!
Now and then a clock begins to chime.
Altho it's late who cares about the time
While it's snowing, blowing,
No one ever think of going.
Pass your glass and pour some more.
Come join the party, shout a hearty
    'Skol!'
Copyright 1948 Robert Music Corp.

Sonja's Rélève

Sonja, Michael and Arthur Treacher in "Countess of Monte Cristo"

Sonja, Michael and Dorothy Hart in a scene from "Countess of Monte Cristo"

On one of our "dates"

Empress of Canada Montreal-Liverpool, June 1951

5

Decade Three 1945-1955

"Today is the first day of the rest of your life." A pleasant idea that can mean almost anything you want it to mean. For me, of course, that day was our wedding day, 23 December 1944; actually it was the beginning of a completely new life. Social and cultural changes began knocking on my door like leaves on a windy day.

In the early 1940s, and certainly by 1944, the glamour of the Golden Era of Hollywood was drawing to a close. But there were still some rigid taboos that had been the hallmark of Hollywood mores and morals. Most actors and actresses did not divulge much of anything of their personal lives, especially their marital status. Most felt and the studios agreed that if they appeared married they would lose much of their sex appeal to the public. So real marriage was discouraged and hidden from the public. A famous story of the period involved Ingrid Bergman. It was discovered that she and her director-lover, Roberto Rossellini, were living together on the island of Stromboli, while both were married to others. She was ostracized by the public, and the industry did not use them in a picture for some time.

With this background, and the attitude of the MGM publicity department, I became concerned that marriage would seriously impede my own progress and success in the film industry.

I discussed this concern with the two men I felt would know and advise me objectively. Billy Grady, who spearheaded my start, and Lew Wasserman, an agent with MCA who had handled the *Ice Follies* when we played in San Francisco and Los Angeles. When I brought up my concern about this they both said exactly the same thing, "Marry the girl!" They had known Norah for some time and knew how valuable she would be for me. My concerns were put to rest, and our plans for the wedding proceeded.

I continued my acting and speech classes at the studio and appeared in a couple of small parts in films. Most of my fellow actors who were on the same schedule took off for the beach as soon as work was done, but I was not so interested in the beach. Of course I was still enamored with the sea, but like most seamen would tell you, if you can't be on a boat or ship, to just be on a beach becomes an almost unbearable envy. One must be on the sea in a vessel, not sitting on its grainy perimeter as fading waves that have already lived douse the feet.

Skating for my own pleasure at the Sonja Henie Ice Palace in Westwood near my small apartment at the Dracker Hotel was a pleasant relaxation and escape from the phoniness of Hollywood life. I was only able to get a small apartment with a single, pull-down bed since housing was so scarce due to the war. Norah left the ice show in New York, had a pleasant visit with her family in Canada, and came out to the coast on the *Super Chief*, the luxury train of the time.

My second picture, *Weekend at the Waldorf*, started just before Norah arrived for our wedding and precluded our having more than a two-day honeymoon. This comedy was to honor one of Manhattan's supreme institutions. The hotel had been built in the 1930s to replace the old Waldorf-Astoria on Fifth Avenue, which was demolished to make room for the Empire State Building. At Park Avenue and 49th, the splashy new 1,800-room Waldorf was the epitome of luxury and *haut monde*. One could arrive by limousine and drive right into the very middle of the inner courtyard, or, to be truly gauche, arrive in one's private railroad car, which was shunted off New York Central's main line into private sidings deep below the hotel. No doubt this was the choice for many low-profile celebrities such as Eisenhower, Nimitz, Winston Churchill, the Astors, and royalty from around the world. Additionally, the likes of President Hoover and the Windsors held permanent residences there. The ballroom, built to be the most magnificent room of any hotel, rose four stories, and the Starlight Roof slid open for moonlight splendor when the weather allowed. Word got out about the immense instruction manual revered by all employees should one wish to maintain employment. As a patron arrives at the front desk, "The clerk's keen appraisal should determine whether to make this transaction efficient, courteous and brief, or make it a dramatic moment for the patron." The forty-seven floor clerks, one to each floor, must say, "Please and thank-you, regularly and sincerely, however talkativeness is bad form and entirely out of place." With this extreme haughtiness, it wasn't hard to imagine Hollywood's desire to make a comedy out of a weekend there. The difficulty was in not crossing the line into the world of mockery. Actually, it was a remake of an old Greta Garbo film called *Grand Hotel* about the famous hotel in Berlin before the war.

So we checked in for our "Weekend at the Waldorf," with a great many stars such as, Walter Pidgeon, Lana Turner, Van Johnson and Ginger Rogers. I was a newly married young officer arriving at the Waldorf, coincidentally, on a two-day leave for a honeymoon. The bride was Judy Collins. In the film we are unable to get a room from the room clerk, but an elderly man overhears this and asks us what we wanted and why. He turns to the room clerk and tells him to give us his suite, as he will be gone for a week. We had a couple of other fun and romantic scenes in the suite, but they were cut because of double entendres that didn't get by the censor's office. It would be fascinating to see them today, as I'm sure the dialogue would appear incredibly mild. But I guess I should be grateful. Mom was proud of my work in that picture, based on just what she saw in the theater and nothing more.

A friend from San Francisco came down for the wedding and could not get a hotel room so I invited him to stay with me, on the couch, for the night before the big day. In the morning when my alarm went off, he encouraged me to hurry and get ready for the big occasion and the start of the rest of my life. I rushed into the shower. When I came out my friend was sitting on the bed looking at his watch with a peculiar look. He claimed there must have been something wrong with my alarm since his watch only showed three in the morning! I checked mine, and it too said three o'clock. I tried to go back to sleep but, of course, that was impossible. I had about four or five hours to figure out the hilarity of his joke. In order to get a marriage license I had to have written permission from my father, not my mother, since I was under twenty-one years old. My father's letter had only come in the day before, so after picking up Norah for the ceremony I had to drive with her and the letter to City Hall to get the license. We got to the church on time. Father Reardon was there, as well as my old boss and now best man, Eddie Shipstad and his wife Lu, Norah's matron of honor, and their son Eddie Joe who was the altar boy. There was a handful, and I mean small handful, of guests from the *Ice Follies* office and there were some from MGM, so it was a very small, intimate wedding. Since the marriage still exists as I write this, apparently there is no direct correlation between depth of budget and depth of love. In the years following that glorious day, I spent many hours explaining this theory to our daughters. It wasn't easy.

After the ceremony Eddie and Lu Shipstad invited us to the Beverly Hills Hotel for a wedding breakfast. At the time I was disappointed they chose a coffee shop for the occasion, until I realized some time later that this was the world famous Polo Lounge! I've never had such a beautiful breakfast in a coffee shop and probably never will again. From there Norah and I went to the Bel Air Hotel. It was not yet famous and in fact had only recently been converted from a horse stable into a motel-like hotel. The bridal suite was, and I believe still is, the only room on the second floor. We spent only two nights there because I had to be at work the day after Christmas on *Weekend at the Waldorf.* I don't remember too much about those two days, except that I undressed for bed and got in my pajamas in the closet, because I was too embarrassed to get undressed in front of Norah. Strange how we were able to conceive eight children. An oddity, but perhaps this is where Norah's fondness for walk-in closets was born.

For our forty-fifth wedding anniversary on 23 December 1989, my friend and boss at *Ice Capades*, George, contacted his friend at the Bel Air Hotel and arranged for us to stay there for the same rate we had paid on our honeymoon in 1944—eleven dollars per day for the bridal suite, which now rents for $350 per day. So that was all we paid!

On Christmas day 1944 we returned to my small apartment at the Dracker with its single pull down bed. After a day or so of trying to both sleep in the single bed Norah thought she should sleep on the couch since I had to work in the morning. In that instant the movie business began to lose its appeal to me. It interfered with my real life, the love of my life.

During the war Hollywood churned out numerous patriotic gung-ho type movies. Producers merely picked up where the western left off. The good guys now wore white tin helmets while the bad guys donned swastika labeled black helmets. Audiences reveled in entertainment that showed we were winning the war complete with bravery, courage and heroics. Even if this was not always the case it certainly sold more tickets. A couple of standouts tried to set the record straight. One was John Ford's *They*

Were Expendable, in which I was cast within a month of our wedding at the top of 1945. It was a fictionalized account about Motor Torpedo Boats at the start of the war in the Pacific, starring John Wayne, and Robert Montgomery, and a new star, Donna Reed. Considered unique at the time, it actually dealt with America's worst military disaster of the war in the Philippines while still paying tribute to the heroic men involved. The picture was under the navy's control, so no wives or family were allowed to visit the set in Florida. The navy took over a hotel in Miami Beach for the cast. Each morning we were taken in the Torpedo Boats to the shooting site on Key Biscayne, which was then an uninhabited coconut plantation not yet connected to the mainland by the causeway. We were there for three months, which was terribly long for a newly married young man! One of my roommates, Blake Edwards, became the famous producer of the *Pink Panther* movies and married Julie Andrews. I was most impressed with Ford's desire for realism and refusal to romanticize history. He allowed us to act as we felt we should in each scene. How could we argue with the man who won the Oscar for best director and an Oscar for *The Grapes of Wrath* just four years earlier. As I think back, his desire for realism and refusal to romanticize history was clearly a winning ticket.

The exuberance of finishing a tough shoot was reduced to great sorrow as we returned to Los Angeles on 15 April at the time of Franklin Roosevelt's funeral. There was great sadness in the country as this marked the first death of a current president since Warren G. Harding. It was also said to be the eve of victory. Indeed within the next three weeks, Hitler committed suicide, Mussolini was assassinated and the Germans surrendered as Europe awoke to freedom. At his funeral it was said Roosevelt "was a hero of the war, and he literally worked himself to death in the service of the American people."

For a number of years after the film, we lived in Newport Beach, California. One night visiting a favorite restaurant we literally bumped into John Wayne, who was leaving as we arrived. I said, "Hi, Duke, Michael Kirby. I was in a movie with you many years ago." He took my hand and stared at me for a moment then said, *"They Were Expendable*, you were in my crew on the PT boat." And he was right. I was one of about six or eight crew members on the boat he skippered. That was a fantastic memory after almost thirty years but just shows what a real man he was and why he was so successful and popular.

With the war over we were now able to move to a regular apartment not far from the center of Westwood Village, and the ice rink. Teaching was becoming *de rigeur* as I realized my MGM contract wasn't keeping me busy on a daily basis. A distinctly different teaching opportunity came to me from the Schramm brothers. Roy and Ray Schramm had been skaters in the *Ice Follies* but had been drafted into the army. After discharge they approached me with two unique ideas: one was financial and the other was illusory. They wanted to create a skating number while chained together at the wrists and ankles. Since they were identical twins, the impression would intensify. And the G.I. Bill of Rights was going to get us there. This bill allocated funds to all veterans for job training and civilian rehabilitation. The Schramms believed their skating lessons should qualify them for this disbursement. The government agreed and allotted sixty-three dollars per month for their training, which I would receive for helping them put the chained number together. After many hours of trial and error both on and off the ice, the number was completed and, to our gratification, taken on by *Ice Follies* as one of their featured numbers.

As the chained number remained popular for many years, Norah and I gained popularity too—even though the 1940 and 1944 Olympics were canceled due to the war,

Sonja's popularity of skating was still in the air. More and more film celebrities and their families were coming to us for lessons. A couple of our favorites were Shirley Temple and Cyd Charisse's daughter, who naturally became very good because of her dancing ability and her mother's fabulous dancing ability, respectively. Jane Powell also became a close friend, and we introduced her to another skater, Gerry Stefen, who had been one of Sonja Henie's skating partners. In fact, based on our introduction, by 1949 Jane and Gerry were married.

About six or seven months into marriage we had what most good Catholics would consider a crisis. Norah had not yet been blessed within! We arranged to go to a doctor for tests to be sure we were physically okay. When the war was in full swing and all factories operated around the clock, there was a problem keeping workers awake so a No-Doz pill had been developed. Workers were urged to take them so they would not fall asleep at their jobs.

At the conclusion of our physical exams the doctor assured us that there was nothing wrong with either of us—well almost. As we were leaving his office he pulled me aside and said, with a broad smile, "Try using some No-Doz pills."

I must have gotten the message because we were pregnant shortly thereafter and our first child, Michael John, was born about seventeen months after our wedding. He was not a "junior," but was named after a brother of Norah's who had drowned as a young three-year-old. The occasion of M.J.'s birth was our first nonbusiness meeting with a movie star. In the room next to Norah's, Georgiana Montalban, Ricardo's wife and Loretta Young's sister, was welcoming their first baby too. When the babies were brought to their mothers for nursing, the husbands were escorted out of the room, apparently the nuns running the hospital thought there was something wrong with a husband watching his wife nursing their own baby! But that was then. So Ricardo Montalban and I were relegated to the waiting room down the hall until the babies finished feeding. It gave me an opportunity to get to know a fine gentleman.

Baby M.J. was an excellent alternative to No-Doz. From day one he was adept at providing the same effect as No-Doz both night and day. So a couple months later when a crying Norah picked me up at work, I wasn't too surprised when she blurted through her tears, "I'm pregnant and I don't want to get fat all over again! Spoken like a true athlete. All I could think of was how could this be? The first one wasn't paid for yet! M.J. was eleven months old when Norah gave birth to his "Irish twin," a delightful little girl, Tricia, who is still a "doll," even though she is a grandmother now too.

When Fernando Lamas first moved to Hollywood from Mexico, he lived on the same block we did in Westwood Village. His daughter Alex was over at our place playing with our children almost daily, and we became quite friendly with Fernando. We had a few other acquaintances through the business, but for the most part we truly felt we did not fit into the social life of the movie people.

This was exemplified at our own New Year's Eve party. I only call it our own because the MGM publicity department told us to refer to it that way. Yet it was entirely their own creation. Norah and I were merely names they could pin with the labels host and hostess. I was still under contract with MGM and they said I needed the publicity. I think it had more to do with our willingness to play Mr. and Mrs. when, as I mentioned earlier, everyone else in Hollywood went to great lengths to conceal their personal lives—especially their marital status.

Trying to play the role of the good guys, we let the party get underway. It was a beautiful, late August evening, just perfect for a New Year's Eve bash. Well, perfect for Hollywood of course. In order for the story and photos to make the December or January editions of the fan magazines, they had to be taken in August. Whatever it takes to fool the public. The studio did all the invitations, and sure enough we did not know a single one of our "guests." I felt like a phony. The photographer would set up "candid" shots.

Now there's an oxymoron. This is where I saw some Oscar-quality performances. It was too bad we had already moved into the era of the "talkies," because after the picture was taken we all retreated to separate areas since we didn't know what to talk to each other about. Those shots had about as much life to them as the tomato-aspic-encrusted liverwurst that the studio caterers brought in. Even the fruitcake was fresher than the conversations we had with some of our "guests."

For us this was typical Hollywood, but now it was on our doorstep. Somehow we just couldn't get comfortable with the idea. This town was a puzzle. Some people can stand out and instantly fit right in the middle. Others are basic four-sided pieces, constantly trying but never neatly fitting, forcing when it doesn't really work. And then somebody says, "I think this piece fell out of another box. Our puzzle doesn't even have this color at all."

I made the best of a few small parts here and there. In 1947 I got a meatier role in *Summer Holiday*. I played Mickey Rooney's older brother, and we were both Walter Huston's sons. This was MGM's attempt to give Mickey a new image, since his Andy Hardy roles were wearing thin. Walter Huston was a fine gentleman who helped me immensely with my acting. The director, Rouben Mamoulian was known as the master behind Jeanette MacDonald's 1932 musical *Love Me Tonight*. A very light film but made memorable by his superb staging of the catchy tune "Isn't It Romantic." He also brought his genius to Fredric March's *Dr. Jeckyll and Mr. Hyde*. A true actor's director, he always told me to justify each action in every scene. In one scene in which I had dialogue with Mickey and then walked through the doorway, the director asked me where I was going when I walked out of the scene. Actually, it was to an empty stage, but he wanted me to know in my mind specifically to what room of the house I was going. Mamoulian tried to explain in his thick accent, "Mikael, you must always have that in mind. Camera must see thought in eyes, that way audience will see purpose in your mien." The film was a critical success but couldn't fill the cinemas as the public just didn't buy a grown-up Mickey Rooney. Regardless, Lennie Hayden, the musical director for the film, threw a cast party to celebrate our reviews. Lennie was married to the beautiful Lena Horne, and we were honored to be invited to their home in Beverly Hills. With Lennie's accompaniment on the piano, Lena sang a few songs, and it was pure magic. I'll always remember it as one of the most pleasant evenings I ever spent in Hollywood.

The summer of 1947 found us driving two thousand miles with two babies to visit our families back in Ontario. Old Route 66 carried us right through the middle of every town. This is very beneficial to someone investigating the percentage of road bordered by farmer's markets versus farmer's cows. And of course the children seemed to be interested in the recurrence and duration of every red light. This was obvious, as they seemed to close their eyes in concentration between intersections. Then, every time I came to a stop, which was incessant, they awakened and cried out as though their red light theory had just been proven.

We did not have air conditioning in our car, so our plan was to drive through the desert at night—although with two babies it is hard to plan anything. We resorted to a new-fangled air conditioning system consisting of a metal cylinder about a foot in diameter and two-feet long with a vent that fit into the top of the right front window. It was filled with straw which we'd soak with cool water, allowing near-frigid air to flow right through it and into our car. It was quite a contraption and very effective—that is, unless you're in the desert, which we were. In a mere five minutes the water completely evaporates and you're back to square one. Perhaps we were stricken with a bit of heatstroke, but at one point the four of us determined that not even baked ziti could retain heat as well as our car did.

Old Route 66 seemed to wind its way into eternity. The children had finally found dreamland, and Norah was sleeping peacefully too. Through the rearview mirror I could barely visualize the last of the silhouetted cactuses as the sun presented its closing rays to Hollywood, I thought of the life back there. Deals had been made that day, pictures had wrapped, and cocktail parties were in full swing. Norah and I had been invited to one that night at Billy Grady's home. I pictured the party back there. Martinis would be prevalent in the smoky salon as glamorous actors discussed such things as projects starting on Monday, casting on future projects not yet determined, and of course, affairs of the heart. And then there was Norah and I, looking like Andy Hardy's family driving across the Midwest. The contrast couldn't have been more extreme. I thought of the bizarre Hollywood business and imagined the columnists in the next day's papers would say, "Everyone who's anyone in Hollywood was there," and then the editor would cut the rest of the sentence, "except Michael Kirby." Right. Let's see, I wonder who would be there. Sonja Henie? Maybe Norah and I could have finally met Sonja Henie. Maybe this was the night. Surely there was Betty Grable politely sitting on the edge of the davenport with her million-dollar legs making up for any shyness. The war was over, and Hollywood movies are now made to be hot. These gals fit the bill like Lana Turner fits her sweaters. Lana would be there fresh off *The Postman Always Rings Twice*. I wonder if she expected to see me since we had worked together just a bit earlier. No, she'd be chatting up the serene Clark Gable. MGM was considering reteaming them. Rita Hayworth, Hollywood's love goddess, was there in a clinging, black satin dress, but she was not clinging to second husband Orson Welles. He wouldn't even be there, and the columns were having a field day with the talk of divorce. Now there was a man who could tell you about Hollywood. Welles, considered a boy genius just ten years earlier, was now described by one critic as 'the youngest living has-been." This title was awarded just for the brilliant *Citizen Kane*'s camouflaged derogatory profile of William Randolph Hearst. What kind of industry was I dabbling in? I looked at my peaceful family and wondered how to spare them from Hollywood's idiosyncrasies.

I could picture Bette Davis standing very erect in "the power corner," cigarette and holder in one hand, goblet in the other. The two-time Oscar winner carried herself with an air of class. It took guts just to begin a conversation with her. Joan Crawford would aggressively work the room in search of the "right" people to chat up. Three years earlier my bosses at MGM considered Joan "washed up." She left for Warner's, jumped on a script that Bette

Davis passed up, and was now an Oscar winner for the last year's *Mildred Pierce*. Joan, at a party, would eventually take a stance in the anteroom in order to pounce on any big bosses arriving.

Barbara Stanwyck, another tigress, felt she was still riding high after *Double Indemnity*. But that was three years before, and this business had proved over and over again how fickle it can be. Why should I have put myself in such a company? I had a wife and children. I felt I was a gentleman, certainly a family man.

Of course I had to admit Hollywood did have plenty of upstanding characters too. Just the past year we had the pleasure of being invited to Shirley Temple's wedding. She found herself a fine gentleman by the name of John Agar. Here was a bonafide movie star marrying an army sergeant who wanted nothing more to do with this business than accompanying his wife to an occasional movie premiere. Another fine gent, Cary Grant was "Notorious" in Hitchcock's thriller in the past year but didn't carry that title with him off the set. And Gene Kelly, hot after declaring to Frank Sinatra, "if you knew Suzy," in *Anchors Aweigh* would just make his customary appearance at the party and then leave. He was not a party fellow. Nor was James Cagney, who had recently appeared in "Dandee" as a Yankee and had the Oscar to prove it.

Now Frank Sinatra, he was another story all together. Despite telling reporters, "Hollywood stinks," he'd be at that party that night. No telling who he'd bring or who he'd go home with, but I could see him there at the bar claiming to be "stag not drag." He'd be lighting some starlet's cigarette and her entire body would begin to smolder. At the other end of the salon and certainly the other end of the spectrum was Humphrey Bogart, the ultimate gentleman. Now Bogey could fuel intense smoldering, but that was on the screen. The public loved Sam Spade, who was "not as crooked as I'm supposed to be." And the screen smoldered two years earlier when Lauren Bacall told him, "If you want me, just whistle." Apparently her drawling explanation, "Just put your lips together and blow," had worked. Bogey would be at the party quietly in the corner with Lauren. A sincere, straightforward romance was being nurtured— something the columnists just can't write enough about. Of course Hollywood has its pleasant moments, too. MGM has turned musicals into a topnotch artform with Carmen Miranda, Garland and Rooney, and Fred Astaire's *Zeigfield Follies* just last year. I could almost picture Crosby and Hope rollicking along Old Route 66 with us. Their *Road* series had been a big hit ever since they claimed, "Like Webster's Dictionary, we're Morocco bound." The last year they took audiences on *The Road to Utopia*. But Sonja Henie? Why hadn't we found Sonja yet? I could see Henry Fonda sitting with best friend Jimmy Stewart, Oscar winner in 1940, and John Ford who won an Oscar for directing Fonda in *The Grapes of Wrath*, also seven years earlier. Ford would continue praising that Fort Apache script, trying to entice Fonda for the lead. Amiable Jimmy would probably be encouraging his friend—there was not a touch of envy, even though Jimmy's career hadn't quite picked up where he had left off before the war. Jimmy had a good run with MGM and Capra, but when he returned from flying missions over Germany, it wasn't to MGM. Capra started his own independent company, and he put Stewart in the last year's critical and box-office flop *It's a Wonderful Life*, but which since became a perennial favorite. I had overheard on the MGM lot that now both Henry and Jimmy wanted to get back to westerns.

For the life of me I just couldn't figure why it flopped. George Bailey seemed like a nice enough fellow. And Donna Reed, well she was as warm and beautiful and sensible as my Norah, now gingerly resting her head on my shoulder. I knew she'd stand by me just like Donna Reed supported George Bailey. But what was I doing? I had a solid plan just a bit before. Make a fortune in skating shows within two years, go back home for a college education, and then delve into the plastics business. Plastics. Well George Bailey was offered a career in plastics too. He turned it down too, and for what—love, travel and a long shot. Maybe we both made the wrong decision. Maybe George and I should both have been sitting in a plastics factory right then. Maybe people would've liked that movie much more. Sure it was a wonderful life all right— as long as one stayed on track. But was eastbound on Route 66 the right path? Or should I have been back there, cocktailing with all the glams and playing the game, the publicity game? One thing I knew for sure, Norah would see me through. According to that year's big Oscar winner, these were supposed to be "the best years of our lives." Well I really couldn't complain so far. Doors had opened for me, and I'd jumped at every opportunity. I had to believe there were more doors, and that they were still going to open for us. I had Norah to guide me. Together we'd strive to make every year the best year of our lives. Until Norah said, "Turn around Michael, it's time for plastics," we'd keep looking for those inviting doors. The honking horn of a speeder jolted me out of my daydream. Norah sat up. "How far along are we?"

"It's about 1:30. Maybe I'll pull into a motel at the next town."

Norah asked what was keeping me awake and I said, just a lot of thoughts about the movie business, thinking about that party we missed tonight, wondering why we haven't met Sonja Henie in Hollywood yet."

Norah responded, "Michael, don't ask for the moon, we have the stars." She curled up again.

It left me speechless. She must have heard everything I'd been thinking the past few hours, and then put her final touch on all my concerns. "Don't ask for the moon, we have the stars," Bette Davis's famous line from *Now Voyager* just five years earlier. Norah, she was a no-nonsense gal, and I loved her more and more every day. I saw a sign for Dot's Diner and Motel. In short order the four of us were tucked in. The babies barely woke through the transfer and must have just figured it was Dad's driving—not quite smooth as ice. I gently caressed Norah and closed my eyes, a welcome relief from near white-line fever.

I sunk deeper and deeper. My entire body relaxed and then I heard it. Doors opening and closing, too many to count. Huge movie arc lights glared down a long hotel corridor with doors on each side. I got nervous because I knew I wasn't in costume. I hadn't gone to make-up yet, and worse, I couldn't find my script. The dialogue I thought I had memorized escaped me. I tried calling out, but even my own vocal cords had deserted me. And the doors. They kept slamming. I ran towards a door and could barely see a cocktail party. I heard laughing and the clinking of ice in glasses. It was a Hollywood cocktail soiree. Frank Sinatra was at the bar. "Hey Kirby," he yelled out, but the door slammed shut. "Hey Kirby," continued to resonate down the hall as I ran to the next door. This door was wide open. The cadence of machinery and a queer odor emanated from the room. People were in odd-looking suits with head gear resembling an H. G. Wells space story.

A gentleman approached me at the doorway and took off his mask. It was Jimmy Stewart. He extended his hand. "Michael, welcome to Sam Wainwright Plastics. We've been waiting for you. I'm George Bailey, and I'd like to show you to your place in the assembly line. Today we're working on buttons for cars so that as soon as someone invents the automobile cooling system, we can provide the button to turn it on." I put my hand out, but it was drawn like a magnet to the door handle. "Cut!" I heard the director yell. "Michael, you're supposed to shake Jimmy's hand and walk in. Let's go again—take two!" Jimmy, undeterred, again said his line. I reached out but was overpowered again. By this time Wainwright had walked over. "George Bailey, what seems to be the problem here? Kirby doesn't want to get in on the ground floor of the plastics industry?"

I yanked on the door, but it didn't budge. All my feet were frozen, and I couldn't utter a sound. "Michael—it's bad enough you showed up late. George here tried to cover for you. You know if we get behind here, Mr. Potter will shut us down, and you'll find yourself on a stool in Martini's Bar, or worse, panhandling around town with that drunken ol' druggist, Mr. Gower, and . . ." The foul odor of the burning plastic made me dizzy, and they continued blaring into my face about Potter and Zuzu's petals. The door handle started burning my hand, but I couldn't loosen my grip. The director yelled, "All right, cut! This isn't working. Kirby. You'd better study that script. Right now you're walking on thin ice!" With that, the door jerked, and for a split second I saw Jimmy Stewart smirking. Then *whoosh*, the door slammed shut, knocking me into the hallway. I took off down the corridor, bellowing, "Norah, Norah, help!" Ahead was a door that a gentle breeze seemed to knock. Standing on the threshold, all I could see was a warm midnight sky complete with brilliant stars and a radiant moon illuminating the ocean below me. A distant lightning storm crackled its electricity on the horizon. With each flash I was able to barely make out what seemed to be a tiny figure that appeared to dance about on the ocean's surface. Another crackle and I could see it was a sprightly blonde. She was skating. With another glinting bolt, this fairy was spinning fast, then abruptly stopped in a rélevé position. Now a meteoric flicker. She was running on her toes across the ocean's smooth surface. Then she arched and stretched one leg into a spiral. A gust of wind threw me forward, and my heels tried to grip the threshold while my toes teetered over the edge. The storm was coming closer, and there was nothing to grasp. My heels began to burn, and the swirling wind teased me as I rocked back and forth. The blond figure continued her dance, when all of a sudden a powerful squall and detonating thunderbolt sent me falling, falling . . .

❧ 6 ❧

The Sonja Henie Legacy

In the late 1800s on the frozen ponds of New York's Central Park, an American dance teacher by the name of Jackson Haines had the idea of transferring dance movements to ice skating. His first attempts, such as dancing bears and circus-type clowns, were too comedic, and the audience in New York did not appreciate this. He took his idea to Europe this time with more serious interpretations of the well-known ballets. Soon he appeared in all major cities that could provide the frozen surface he needed. Warmly received by European audiences, they returned their appreciation by bestowing Haines with the title "The American Skating Prince." Europe, particularly Vienna, was considered the world center for the art of true figure skating, which, as its name implies, involved the intricate drawing of figures on the ice with skate blades. These drawings were originally based on the figure eight and then evolved into convoluted patterns of more than one hundred different designs. What made Haines so different was that he was more concerned with the positions and movements of the body while performing these designs than the etchings the blade left behind. It was considered so unique that in deference to his American background, it became known as the International Style of Figure Skating.

In the late nineteenth century, when Haines was touring Europe and spending much time in Scandinavia, particularly Norway, a little girl named Selma, who was later to become Mrs. Wilhelm Henie and the mother of a girl named Sonja Henie, fell in love with Jackson Haines and more importantly with the beauty of skating that he developed. She vowed that someday she would have a child that would be the best at that style of skating. Selma was blessed with a son named Leif and a vibrant little girl named

Sonja. As soon as they could walk they were introduced to fancy skating.

And skate they did. Sonja seemed to have a natural flair for the sport. An eleven-year- old Sonja was a last place finisher in the 1924 Olympics. But determination and perseverance brought her a World Championship title just three years later. The following year, 1928, in St. Moritz, her passion for the art based on Jackson Haines's style brought her the Olympic gold medal. Selma and Papa Henie couldn't have been more proud.

Five World Championship titles later, and now with the 1932 Olympic gold medal around her neck, this little girl was about to leave her mark on the sport that no one else could ever surpass. By 1936 with a total of ten World Championship titles to her name and an unprecedented third Olympic gold medal, it was clear to Mama Henie, Papa, and Leif, that Sonja was about to take on the world. By now Sonja herself would have been hard-pressed to see it any other way. Thank you Jackson Haines and thank you Mama Henie.

Fate Again and the Fateful Meeting

The fall of 1947 found us back in Westwood Village, California fulfilling my contract with MGM. I still had many hours to myself, which I spent at the Sonja Henie Ice Palace teaching and skating for my own benefit and pleasure. One afternoon as I got off the ice and walked past the manager's small office, I noticed his door was halfway open. I paused just to wave but then stopped dead in my tracks as I heard, "Hey Michael, would you like to meet Sonja Henie?" I took two steps back toward his voice and found myself on the threshold of his open doorway. All I could think was, "finally." He went on to explain she skated every morning by herself and was now interested in a new partner. My mind flashed back to the nightmare at Dot's Diner and Motel. The manager continued on, but my thoughts drowned him out. I felt, again, I was teetering, and so I placed my hand on the door frame. I looked down, half expecting to see that same vast ocean and the blonde nymph dancing on the horizon. The manager droned on about Sonja and now I knew who that sprightly blonde was in the nightmare. This was it. The door that was about to radically impact my life was wide open and I was no longer wavering back and forth while hanging on. Finally. This time I didn't need a squall or even a gust of wind. I was ready to jump right in without a lifejacket.

"You skate like a Canadian," Sonja said matter-of-factly as we stroked around together. Unsure of how to take that, I decided to be flattered and proudly declared, "Well I am Canadian." I was relieved to see her flash that trademark dimpled smile as she responded that one of her best partners had been a Canadian. I knew she meant Stewart Rayburn, who had taught her one of her most popular numbers, the tango on ice. Feeling more comfortable, I held Sonja a bit tighter around the waist to better synch our stroking. "Canadians extend their leg at the end of every stroke whether we going fast or slow, yah?" she asked in her engaging Norwegian accent. I had never realized that before and was impressed with Sonja's perception. Now I pushed harder to increase our speed and perhaps enhance our flow. I thought of Sonja's comment and glanced at her stretched free leg. I was instantly reminded of the uproar she caused when she took to the ice at her first World Championships. When the norm for ladies was black skates, black stockings and heavy skirts down to the ankle, out stepped Sonja, to everyone's aghast. She wore a skirt so short her knees were visible, and every time she jumped, spun, or even raised her stocking-covered leg above the knee, the skirt would fly up, revealing even more of her now famous legs. Additionally, she had what was thought to be incredible gall for wearing pure white skates. This, she told the press, was because it reminded her of the beautiful snow in her homeland of Norway. I had heard of all these stories and of her flamboyant Jackson Haines style—all in an effort to make skating more entertaining.

By now Sonja was completely responsible for converting skating to an art form with her innovations in show skating that created the professional touring ice show.

Our stroking began to feel as smooth as butter, and I pushed on, feeling more and more confident. This was such an amazing opportunity and I could even feel Sonja becoming more comfortable in my arms. "Okay, Michael, now we do a couple of ice dances. Let's start with Ten Step, yah?" We started, and before the first turn I felt this so-called amazing opportunity slip through my hands, now like dripping melted butter. We were doing a simple turn around each other called a mohawk, when my blade caught hers and I tripped her. I tripped Sonja Henie! But thank heavens for experience, I was able to catch her just before she hit the ice. Sonja put her arms around me and her head on my shoulder. "If you can do that, you can do anything with me." A dubious response to be sure, but spoken in innocent broken English. With my mind set on a career with a new partner, I took that to mean just one thing—I was hired.

We rehearsed every day together, trying more and more difficult moves as we began to make up numbers for the new tour scheduled to go out in the fall. Sonja decided we should do three pair numbers in this show. It was quite a compliment, since she usually did only one number with a partner. We were scheduled to rehearse for six weeks before going on the road.

I thought my work with *Ice Follies* was extensive, but as Sonja and I became more friendly both on and off the ice, I realized my show skating experience paled in comparison to hers. Even back during the time of her first Olympic title, she was doing exhibitions at amateur ice carnivals put on by the most prestigious skating clubs in Toronto, Boston, New York, and Philadelphia. In addition to these appearances, she performed during the intermissions of hockey games. It was while doing this that she met Arthur Wirtz of Chicago. He owned arenas in Chicago, Detroit, St. Louis, and had ownership interest in Madison Square Garden and hockey teams that played those arenas. At that time there were more show skaters in Europe. They had a number of small ice rinks in night clubs and hotels, and Sonja was familiar with many of those skaters since they had been her contemporaries during her competitive days. With her charisma and persuasive powers, she was able to convince Wirtz that she could obtain enough skaters to perform an abundance of interesting skating that would entertain a stadium filled with Americans for an entire evening. Wirtz decided to give her a chance and in the spring of 1936 the *European Ice Revue* was born. I knew of this show because my old bosses had gotten their start with Sonja's show. Eddie and Roy Shipstad and their partner, Oscar Johnson, learned the tricks of the trade on this tour before they started the *Ice Follies*. Another cast member was a champion speed skater by the name of Bess Earheart, and she later became Roy's wife. Her retirement gave Norah the starring role in *Ice Follies*, and it included an obligation to pair skate with none other than me. Clearly we had come full circle. But back in 1936, Sonja's plans to take on the world had only just begun.

Rehearsing with Sonja was a joy. Her determination to get it right was unflappable. This passion is how she was able to transform her championship titles into a form of entertainment that no one else dreamed possible. Her innovations in show skating were the spark needed to create the professional touring ice show that we see today. And she fought for it every step of the way; it was no lucky chance. I began to see that she was relentless in her desires. But today's rehearsal was cut short as her secretary, Dorothy Stevens, came to the rink railing to remind Sonja she had to get going in order to get to her next appointment on time. "Yah Michael, you must come with today, I have a proposition for you, okay?" Sonja's English was not always entirely perfect, but at this point the idea of a "proposition" from Sonja would have made me rather flappable.

I knew Sonja had been meeting with Wirtz to discuss a new film she was planning the next year. Today she wanted me to escort her to a meeting with the film's producer, John Beck. Dorothy drove us and on the way Sonja was determined to bring me up to date on her movie career. She spoke in a manner that made me think I should be taking notes. I didn't have to. I had heard tidbits over the years, but for some reason now Sonja really wanted me in on her life.

Sonja pragmatically explained that after her 1930 World Championship title in New York she met Franklin Roosevelt, then governor of New York. When Lake Placid hosted the 1932 Olympics which Sonja won—Roosevelt, then favored to become the U.S. president, treated Sonja as if she were the only guest in town. He was so taken with her that he invited her to his summer home, Campobello, an island off the coast of Maine. Sonja smirked when she put her hand on my knee and looked me in the eye when she said, "We soon became very close friends. You see, Michael, you stick with me because I know how to make this country work for us." Of course, that day in the car I did not realize the depth of truth in what Sonja was telling me. But in the years since stories have surfaced from reliable sources of Roosevelt being surrounded with mistresses. He even had them stay in the White House.

With that accomplishment in her back pocket, Sonja went on to explain how she convinced William Randolph Hearst to put stories about her on the entertainment pages, not just the sports pages, of his newspapers. Sonja then took out a full-page ad in his Los Angeles paper to announce her own ice show at a small dingy arena on Van Ness Avenue in Hollywood called Polar Palace. She told me her objective was to attract the attention of Hollywood producers, and she knew Hearst had many connections there since his current mistress was the great star of the day, Marion Davies. Naturally that ad got for me the attention of Darryl Zanuck. "Michael you know, right? Dear Darryl, head of Twentieth Century Fox Studio?" Of course I knew Zanuck's title. I had just never heard of him referred to as "Dear Darryl." But with Sonja's delightful accent, it never sounded lascivious, even though Zanuck had an "interesting" reputation with women. Again she put her hand on my knee, looked me in the eye, and said, "Michael, Dear Darryl offered me a skating number in one of his musical features. This made me laugh, so I *pursueveered*, Michael (she had a knack for combining words such as pursue and persevere. Those being two of her best talents, one would have thought she would know each of those words backwards and forwards. Or maybe with Sonja's foxhunt technique, it really should be just one word on its own. Regardless, I was beginning to understand her better and better each day, and I couldn't help but be reminded of the day she said, "Michael you can do anything with me." Okay, so she *pursueveered*, and my prize was Dear Darryl giving me my own film called *One in a Million*.

Now this part of the story I knew. Wirtz's *European Ice Revue* was a huge success its first year out, so Wirtz had the cast agree to return in the fall for another tour. Meanwhile, Zanuck's *One In A Million* became a smash hit. Sonja, now living in Hollywood with Mama Henie and Papa, could see herself easily ascending the ladder of success. Finally, on the turf she dreamed of, Sonja decided to step up to the next rung by telling Wirtz she would only return to his ice revue in Chicago if he changed the name to *Sonja Henie's Hollywood Ice Revue*. Wirtz's income from Sonja was skyrocketing, and he knew this was only the tip of the iceberg so he had no problem agreeing with Sonja and booked the show in every arena he controlled. Who would've thought one could find gold nuggets on an iceberg? But Wirtz foresaw his fortune and knew Sonja was fast becoming one of his most profitable gold mines.

However, that same summer Shipstads and Johnson had started their own show, *Ice Follies*, with their star, Bess Earheart. Obligated to return to Wirtz's *Ice Revue* in the fall, they got over their rift by jumping on the whirlwind of publicity and publicizing their show and Bess Earheart as *Two in a Million*.

Here I was walking into yet another Hollywood producer's office, this time with the distinction of escorting a woman who, within a few years, had already taken Hollywood by storm. Ten years earlier, Sonja became one of the highest paid stars, averaging sixteen thousand dollars a week per film. This turned out to be more than double her asking price when she arrived there after her 1936, and final, Olympic title. Her father, a wealthy furrier, had given her a keen business sense and even though Hollywood originally balked at her demand of seventy-five thousand dollars per film, Zanuck's gamble on *One in a Million* paid off for all involved. One year later Twentieth Century Fox amended her contract: five years, three pictures a year at $160,000 per picture. That same year, at thirteen years old, I came in fifth in a class of five junior men at the Canadian Nationals! Was I honored to be asked to sit in on this meeting? Absolutely. Did I know why I was asked to sit in on this meeting? Absolutely not.

"Michael, we're aware that you have been rehearsing with Miss Henie for some time now, and we've also seen your screen test at MGM," began the producer Beck.

I thought, "Oh no, not the personality test."

"And we've seen your work in your recent pictures."

Okay, so it was another small part to add to my collection.

"Michael would you consider playing the leading man in Sonja's next picture?"

Of course I was completely surprised and wholly flattered. This would be a first. No other skating partner had ever played Sonja's leading man. I could hardly wait to call Norah.

Unfortunately, any great deal always contains something in the fine print that one should never overlook. As far as Wirtz was concerned, we merely had a verbal agreement. He produced Sonja's ice show and was also a partner in her movie productions. Our verbal contract was verbally renewed every year for the next seven. It was never a problem, but always unusual. But Sonja again had her own technique. She liked to have the fine print not on paper and not verbal, but rather in her own mind and it would only become verbal when one least expected it.

Before we were to go into production on the movie, our priority was to get this show put together and complete the tour. That meant costume fittings, which Sonja decided should take place in New York. Sonja wanted to have a choice of colored costume so she could choose a color for each performance that matched her mood of that day. So before every performance I had to check with her to find out which color we wore today. Interestingly, I thought my costume fittings had already been completed there in Los Angeles, but Sonja said, "No, no, no, no, Michael. You must escort me to New York. We must show the costumer how you hold me and how you lift me, yah? If we don't do this perhaps I lose the costume one night on the ice, you see?"

Well. Interesting couple of choices Miss Henie presents isn't it? I either, as a married man, escort a woman to New York in order to hold her or endure a performance where this same woman ends up revealing herself one night, again as I hold her. A bit extreme I thought. Sonja always had a way of painting a most interesting picture, but truly she should have stuck with abstract art. In reality Sonja's scenario of a disastrous outcome was highly unlikely. Regardless, given the two options, I chose to stick with my business partner and travel together on a business trip to New York in a businesslike manner.

As I had done so many times already, I chose to believe her English had slightly failed her, and again somehow Sonja came up with an inaccurate Norwegian translation. Certainly, I was not going as an escort.

My last transcontinental flight was in 1945 for the film *They Were Expendable*. It took eleven hours. For the forty passengers, this was considered an incredible feat, since prewar transcontinental flights in a DO could take up to sixteen hours. But Sonja and I boarded the new Lockheed Constellation. Powered by four Pratt and Whitney engines, along with fifty passengers and a crew of six, we whisked off to New York in a mere seven hours. Commercial aviation was finally taking off and quite literally flying high. The level of comfort on these new planes was tremendous. Sonja and I were able to slightly recline in upholstered seats. There was greatly improved sound proofing, steam heat or air conditioning, electrical outlets, and of course the essential cabin pressure which enabled us to fly at a greater altitude resulting in a swift speed of 312 miles per hour. I figured with commercial aviation becoming so prevalent, Sonja must be traveling back to Norway as often as possible. Surely her shows would be huge successes in her homeland. However, the story Sonja told me could not have been a more extreme polar opposite.

The 1936 Olympics took place in Garmisch-Partenkirchen, Germany. Sonja, already a two-time Olympic champion had announced this would be her last Olympic competition. She was already incredibly popular and needed police escorts, whether in the States or in the beautiful cities of Prague and Berlin, where she liked to train. The pressure of wanting to retire as a three-time Olympic champion, caused Sonja great tension. In fact, I had heard a story from a coach that when the results for the compulsory figures were posted with Sonja only 3.6 points ahead of the second place competitor, Sonja, in a bit of a fit, announced it was a misrepresentation and tore the offending score sheet off the board. Then, when her competitor went out to perform her freestyle, the wrong music began. It took some time to find the correct record, and even then the poor girl was flustered and did not skate her best. Sonja, skating last, took to the ice with some hesitancy but eventually overcame her nerves, and her vitality shined through for a winning performance. I saw parts of this in Leni Reifenthal's film, *Triumph of the Will.* I also saw Sonja clearly smiling up at Adolph Hitler and giving the Nazi salute just as so many other competitors had done. Most competitors gave the Nazi salute, at the end of their performance if Hitler or a high official was present, but in Sonja's case, after her salute, which we have on film, she skated over to Hitler and offered her hand, which he brought to his lips like a lovesick boy. But there was something in that smile that went beyond her normal charisma. I also have film of Sonja serving drinks and food to guests as though she was the hostess at a party at Hitler's private retreat in the After mountains at Bergestraten. She was definitely more than a passing competitor!

In the new book by Toller Cranston (former Canadian champion and outstanding innovator in the skating world), *Zero Tolerance* (McClelland and Stewart Inc., the Canadian Publishers), Toller tells of attending a dinner party at a swank Fifth Avenue Penthouse with a number of theatrical and other show business people. When he asked if anyone knew that Sonja Henie had given the Nazi salute to Hitler at the 1936 Olympics, it started such a heated discussion (since someone claimed, erroneously that Sonja was part Jewish) that it broke up the party with most people leaving before dinner was finished! Toller mentions Sonja a number of times in his book, including his respect for her innovations which he felt he was following.

A stewardess brought Sonja her bourbon and water. She placed a hand on my knee, like she so often did for salient points, and began, "Michael, I will tell you why I will not go back to that country, my own country." She did not look me in the eye, but I could see there was great hurt in her face, and her hand on my knee was tense with anger. For the first time I thought Sonja looked old, or maybe she just looked her age for the moment, thirty-six—belying her usual twinkling eyes and dimpled smile that easily took a decade off that number.

Sonja explained that after the 1936 Games, "Adolph" was quite taken with her, and she with him. I did not need more explanation than that, for I already knew of Sonja's ways and abilities with men such as Roosevelt, Zanuck, and Hearst. She went on to say that during a "sweet téte-a-téte with Adolph" (once again I was thrown by her ease in calling these famous and infamous men by their first names) she was able to receive some information. In Sonja's limited English, I was unable to discern if Sonja *pursueveered* him with the goal of attaining information or if their chemistry was undeniable and the information was simply a by-product. Either way, Sonja returned to Norway with a monumental tidbit of war-play potential history-making tidbit hidden in her back pocket.

"I went straight to that demon Quisling, damn him, may he rest in hell," Sonja quipped as she raised her glass to *skol* with her imagined long lost countrymen. I learned that Vidkun Quisling was a Norwegian army officer who tried in vain to launch the Fascist movement in Norway. The country was traditionally neutral, even though the Germans assiduously sought for ties with her. Sonja, with goodwill in her heart, decided to reveal her tidbit of "warplay" but was unfortunate in who was to be the recipient." In 1939 I told to Quisling that Adolph was planning to "liberate" Norway and then France early in next year. That man would not believe me and threaten to expose me and ruin me. He called me *dar gokken gol* and worse names. Kept telling me all Scandinavia is neutral and will remain that way—why would I start such a story to put such fear in our people? He promised to me he would tell his superiors but he never did. I should have known. This was the first man who I could not read. He had evil in his eyes Michael, but I could not read it as revenge against his own country, a coup d'etat in his plan. When I could have done so much for my Norway, and now I am not even welcome there." Sonja's voice started to break, but she turned toward the window and gathered strength from the billowing clouds freely roaming their sky.

Sonja finished her drink and rang for the stewardess to bring her another. I knew there was more to the story but certainly didn't want to encourage her. I could see the anguish was almost unbearable for her, but she had such strength and determination to get beyond it all. That was her nature, and no one incident could ever steal that from her soul.

Just as Sonja had said, on 9 April 1940 at 4:15 in the morning, German naval forces rushed upon each and every main port of Norway. The Norwegians were taken by surprise much like the Americans were in Pearl Harbor the following year. All the ports fell except Oslo, which was taken by troops from the air, and the capitol was abruptly swept into German hands. For two and a half days the Germans worked feverishly, readying all ports and airfields for the arrival of strong support squadrons. By 10 April fighters and bombers were operating from every strategic point along the once pristine coastline of majestic fjords. After losing two British ships, the Allies made a feeble attempt by landing troops at three points. They were too late, too few, and too dispersed to make an impact. The Germans could have laughed at these British who were without armored vehicles, field artillery, and aircraft. Clearly no match for the well-coordinated Germans, the Brits were forced to retreat.

"Knowing from Adolph that Norway was to be first, I called my housekeeper. 'Put Adolph's photograph on the piano in the foyer and leave it there,' I told her." Sonja was given a large photo of Hitler and I was almost sickened to hear of the inscription: "To my darling Sonja, Love Adolph." I downed the rest of my drink. Sure enough, when the German officers commandeered all the large houses for their personal use, Sonja's home was never touched. The housekeeper relayed to Sonja, "The German officers came in, saw the picture, said, 'Heil Hitler,' turned around, and left the house alone." They never touched it during their occupation. I thought to myself that even at 312 miles per hour this was becoming a very, very long flight indeed. Could this story get any worse for Sonja?

"Then they all turned on me, my fellow Norwegians, they started all the stories: Sonja is a traitor, she had romance with Hitler, she doesn't care about us, only cares about making her fortune in America, she sits pretty in her big American home while all of us suffer under Hitler, our country in ruins, but no, not the Sonja Henie home in countryside. She is not our Olympic champion, not our fancy skater, she is a traitor, and lower than even Quisling."

Obviously the Norwegians were never made aware of Sonja's attempt to help Norway resist Hitler by being ready for his invasion. But they were told of her romance with Hitler. Pictures had surfaced of Hitler's famous retreat at Bergestaden in the Alps, which showed Sonja acting as a hostess at one of Hitler's parties. This was more than they could bear and only added fuel to the fire.

To watch Sonja relive this nightmare was like watching a gazelle being brought down by a jaguar. But she was born to be a survivor, and through sheer diligence she may have lost her herd, if you will, but she still had her life. Even though the scars from her loss were now like open wounds as she spoke. In my day-to-day life I considered the war to be behind us. It was over, and we should all be grateful for the heroes who got us through it. The war in Europe was five years, eight months, and six days of hell, and for so many it continues to be hell. But in the States life was looking good once again, and I really didn't want to think about the past. Other than families who lost loved ones, it was difficult to comprehend the plight of people still affected by the war. In my defense, I really had not come close enough to taste the horrors of it. But here was Sonja, serving me an entree of its lifelong effects on someone who, like me, never even set foot on the brutal turf.

Sonja stirred her drink with her finger, seeming mesmerized by the ice going around and around. "That man was colder than the Barents Sea and with no heart like . . . how do you say Michael, you have the farm man made of straw?"

"You mean scarecrow?" I offered.

"Yah, that is the man, made of nothing, no heart, no mind, and he tried to soak my people in his Nazi propaganda. But strong Scandinavians wouldn't hear of it. Then Adolph . . ." Her voice escaped her, lost in her drink as she couldn't find the words to convey her loathing.

I can remember Winston Churchill's speech in 1942 as he said, "A vile race of quislings, which will carry the scorn of mankind down through the centuries." Now I felt like I knew the inside of this man named Quisling. He was the traitor, not Sonja. At the time Sonja went to Quisling, he had already shown Hitler his detailed plans for a coup d'etat in Norway. But Hitler, in order to camouflage his own plans for Norway, was reluctant to discuss Quisling's scheme. By 1942 Quisling was not only spreading Nazi propaganda to his homelands' churches and schools, but he even started an anti-Semitic program and sent about a thousand Jews to their deaths in concentration camps. When Sonja risked everything to go to Quisling, it was he who actually tried to collaborate with Hitler. But for this he finally paid the price. The postwar Norwegian government tried him for treason, and on 24 October 1945, just four months after Hitler's suicide, Quisling was executed. I couldn't help but think that Sonja not being welcome in her own country after all she did was just as big a price to pay.

The captain announced we had started our descent as the skyscrapers and lights of New York City slowly came into view. Sonja was glued to the window. "Michael look, the Empire State Building"—her vivacity had returned—"and there's Central Park!" The plane banked left as we made a smooth declining turn toward Idlewild Airfield. Sonja, still tight to the window, reached for my arm. Her voice softened, "Michael can you see this, it's Ellis Island, and there's the Statue of Liberty, isn't she grand?" Sonja was so anxious to live life to its fullest, so determined not to let anything stifle her spirit. It was clear to me now why in 1941 Sonja Henie became a U.S. citizen.

The Pierre Hotel was always Sonja's choice of residence while in New York. Right in the heart of Manhattan at 59th and 5th Avenues, it bordered the greenery of Central Park, the steeple-topped Sherry-Netherland and the famous massive French chateau, the Plaza. For Sonja, the Pierre, replete with its mansard roof forty floors above the ground, was *the* place to stay. Simply put, she wouldn't have it any other way. And on this trip Sonja was especially adamant about the Pierre because, as she so bluntly put it, "Clark is staying there, and you know Michael, I'm working on him, yah?" Next thing I knew, the three of us were having dinner in Clark Gable's suite. Why I was "work"? She quickly stood on tiptoes, surprised me with a kiss on the cheek, and said, "Tak"—a Scandinavian thank-you. And I now realized that under all that strength there was indeed a very vulnerable young woman who needed a man by her side, even if it was just for support.

The rest of the week was entirely work-related, even the lengthy evenings. Sonja's theory was that if we were to be romantic leads in the film next year, we must be seen as a romantic couple off the ice too. I became accustomed to this back in

Westwood, since Sonja often threw elaborate parties at her home and expected me to show up without Norah. There were times when I obliged but more out of need than agreeing with Sonja's theory. So I'd play the Hollywood game with the hopes of enhancing my career. But more often than not it was because Norah was exhausted from running after two toddlers while another was on the way. Good nannies were expensive, and there were limited numbers of them in this affluent town, so I figured whatever it took to get us closer to our goal would be sufficient. It had nothing to do with a change of heart or morals.

Evenings in New York were a literal tour of each and every swank night club. "Michael, we are to be seen, yah?" So off we went to participate in what was known in New York as the Café Society. We'd dine at Tony's Trouville, the "in spot" of the season, Sardi's on West 44th, the well-known, loud dinner spot for the Broadway crowd, or Toots Shor's where we were likely to bump into Joe DiMaggio. But as always, Sonja had her favorites.

The Stork Club on "the avenue" at 53rd was a publicity seeker's dream come true. It was owned by Sherman Billingsley or "Sherm" to his status-seeking customers, the Stork Club was to the gossip columns like Rockefeller was to money. Sherm had two teams of press agents—a day shift and an evening shift to cover anyone of note who ventured beyond the club's top-hatted stork murals outside its doors. Newspaper columnist Walter Winchell called the up-market speakeasy "the New Yorkiest place in town" and spent every evening at his own table fifty. Sherm also claimed that the elite of the world graced his tables. And he was not boasting. The Duke and Duchess of Windsor, Charles de Gaulle, Ernest Hemingway, Glenn Miller, Prince Aksel of Denmark, and Humphrey Bogart had all been written up in Leonard Lyons's column, "The Lyons Den." But as likely as Sherm was to allow any quality resume or noble bloodlines to walk through his doors he was just as likely to be selective with his company. Elliot Roosevelt, the president's son, was considered to be a black sheep and the Maharajah of Jaipur was refused entry based solely on grounds of color. Such was the thought process in the 1940s.

Sonja was also especially fond of the Champagne Room at El Morocco, complete with its tiger stripe banquettes. She loved the grandness of these banquettes as she sat in the power corner determined to be the focal point of the entire evening. Unlike Sardi's, El Morocco was flashy with socialites. Even *The New Yorker* reported that, "The dress-for-dinner contingent is making its last desperate stand." And this fit Sonja to the tee. I had never known anyone to travel with as much luggage as Sonja. Every outing seemed to rival the fashionably adorned mannequins of Bonwit Teller, Bergdorf Goodman, Lord and Taylor, and Saks Fifth Avenue—all located on the Avenue, of course. Sonja was always in the swim, with the latest in furs, the most vogue hat, distinctly tilted, and jewels that appeared to be a walking billboard for Tiffany's or her favorite, Van Cleef and Arpels.

These evenings had a dual effect for Sonja. In her opinion, they were the essential publicity move that she controlled without the usual entourage of publicist, manager, and agent. But the more I got to know Sonja, the more I could see that these evenings were as essential to her career as they were to her ego. And it was almost understandable. Inside this unyielding woman was a heart that was being slowly crushed by an unrequited love. And this was from a husband of five years already. Sonja had married Dan Topping in 1943. He was the heir to a huge fortune his grandfather and father made in tin mining, but most of it was in a trust his mother controlled. So it was certain that Sonja did not marry him for his money, and besides, she had plenty of her own. Did she marry him merely for his social connections? One might think so. However, when Dan went into the Marines during the war, Sonja lived on base with him when she was not on tour. That has to spell love. Seeing Sonja in the power comer of the Champagne Room was quite the antithesis of the great Sonja Henie living at Quantico Marine Base in Richmond, Virginia. Sonja claimed that one morning for breakfast she used up Dan's entire month's ration of butter just to make hollandaise sauce for eggs benedict. A loving gesture that turned into quite a spat, I'm sure. But it wasn't like Sonja was another Gracie Allen. It was just she would do anything to please her man. She learned this very early on.

In talking with her about our competitive accomplishments I learned the story of her very first competition at age seven as she sat with her parents and brother on benches by the outdoor, homespun rink: "They announced, '*Og dem vinner en . . . Sonja Henie!*' Mama and Leif started clapping, but Papa picked me up in his huge arms, ran me down to ice, and threw me over the railing so I could go out to get my prize. When they put the medal around my neck, I looked back at Papa. I'll never forget. Papa was not clapping or yelling, but he had biggest smile I have ever seen."

As her father stood there frozen but bursting with pride, in Sonja's childlike mind, she instantly knew this was the route to his heart. Like a youngster's first taste of ice cream, the resulting feeling was quite addictive. And over the years as Sonja excelled, her needs were nicely met until she lost her beloved father at her tender age of twenty-five. Tender in Sonja's mind because she had just made her first movie, *One in a Million*, earned more than $200,000 that year, which would be comparable to Julia Roberts's twenty million per picture in today's economy. And she wanted so for her father to see this was not the apex of her career. It was to be merely the beginning. The void in her heart was so great, not even cheering audiences at her sold-out shows could leave her content. For the rest of her life she strove to find that same feeling. Sonja needed to please a man as well as have a man on her arm who would be incredibly proud of her accomplishments. And the last accomplishment was never quite as good as the potential of the next one. This business acumen was engrained by her father, and his success proved the richness of his thought process. And so began Sonja's quest to replace the tender relationship with her father.

I understood now why Sonja needed to be seen at the hottest spots. On the outside she wanted to prove that she needed nobody. She could run the show on her own, precisely the way her father ran his very successful business. While on the inside she was yearning to be something special to one man, the way she had been for her father. She needed to feel the reflection of his pride, and that was the addiction.

Unfortunately, her prowess trampled her fragile interior. Sonja could become quite boisterous and demonstrative, which was part of the cover. One time I recall I had been served a steak, and Sonja asked me, "Is it cooked to satisfaction, Michael?" She was very particular about her entrées so I honestly answered that it was a bit well done. Well arms flew, fingers snapped, and the maitre d' rushed over with waiters in tow. I tried to explain it was adequate, but Sonja, wanting to prove her prowess once again and this time in front of an entire restaurant, persisted while shoving the plate under the maitre d's nose. Now she had gone too far. Escort or not, I refused to be reduced to a boy. I stood up, retrieved my plate and calmly declared, "Sonja, I will eat it just the way it is." Sonja's jaw dropped so far I only wished I had a piece of steak cut that I could have instantly placed in her mouth.

I was an old-fashioned male, and if she wanted me to play the game with I was going to set some ground rules too. For instance, I would not let Sonja pick up a check and insisted on paying them myself. She eventually told Wirtz about this. I can only imagine how that conversation went. Wirtz called one day and laughingly told me to submit expense accounts for reimbursement. That became, in essence, our "Gentlemen's Agreement," the last year's Oscar-winning movie. I really had no choice. Incredibly, Sonja always ordered the best and most expensive item on any menu. When it came to tips, Sonja was a waiter's lottery ticket. And the highlight of her evening would be ordering champagne for the entire orchestra. Not satisfied to be just queen of the ice or just a movie star, Sonja needed to be seen as royalty, wherever she went. She thrived on that and I knew why. But I always thought that deep down, she must have appreciated my strength too, because ever since that steak dinner, we got on just swimmingly. And each night on tip-toes, she reached to my cheek with a sincere "Tak, Michael," an appreciative small kiss and retreat into her room. A quick glimpse of that other side of Sonja, the real side, and I knew I was needed, if for no other reason than to see she was home safely. I was reminded of the first time we skated together when I caught her after a misstep and Sonja had said, "If you can do that, you can do anything with me." At this point I thought she was absolutely right. I could let her succumb to the pitfalls of the business, or I could watch over her and keep her in line. Of course I chose the latter.

So yes, I played the game to its fullest. In fact, I had become exactly what I strove not to be—"an escort." Although in my mind I had to believe in the original sense of the word and not its negative connotation. I was Sonja's escort, and there was nothing salacious about it. I could see through Sonja's promiscuity and trusted her vulnerability. That was really the woman. I knew I could hold her and entertain her and, in short, look like that couple she wanted us to portray, and still go home guilt-free. Surely, I could play the game as well as Sonja could. But what I didn't realize was that this Norwegian lass had her own definition of "the game."

We began three weeks of intense rehearsals in Indianapolis where the show was to open. "Michael, I prefer to have your indivisible attention here so our show can start on the both feet nicely, yah, so Norah must be home in Westwood with the children and we can have successful tour." To put it mildly and in English, undivided attention meant my budding family was not encouraged to see our tour start on the right foot. Well maybe Sonja had a good point. Hotel life on the road does not exactly paint the picture of a house with a white picket fence. And besides, this tour was crucial to our movie career. Additionally, Sonja was definitely placing her "indivisible attention" on the ice, as Dan Topping was nowhere to be seen. Actually, this was not unusual. I still had yet to meet the man.

As we kicked off a very successful opening, we began to fall into Sonja's prescribed daily routine. We were to sleep until about noon, and then Dorothy Stevens would take us to the arena for a two-hour practice. I believe part of what made Sonja's show so alive was her desire to improvise during practice. This was her way of staying fresh, even though we already had numbers set. She would ask the pianist to play popular songs or her favorite, "Almost Like Being in Love," and we would just free dance to the music. Tantamount to ballroom dancing, Sonja would let me lead as the music seemed to carry us across the ice. Almost daily we discovered a particular move by accident that we could incorporate into one of our numbers. This being just one aspect of her work ethic, was definitely one of the keys to Sonja's success.

Skating with Sonja, after I got over my early nervousness of working with an Olympic champion and movie star, became quite a game. She chatted endlessly during the pair numbers but never stopped smiling. She would always comment on the size of the house, (audience capacity) and if she saw empty seats (which she could spot even up in the balcony) she swore at the manager or advertising people. Sometimes in her delightful Norwegian accent she grandly sang the lyrics of our encore number. It was a piece called, "I Don't Know Why I Love You Like I Do," and it included a line, ". . . the only time you hold me is when we're dancin'. . ." At that point Sonja would look me in the eye with her effervescent smile and change the word "dancin'" to "skating." At first I enjoyed her seemingly capricious nature but as the nights went on that look became an extended pause. It was all I could do to lead her into the next move as her continuing gaze seemed to beg for an explanation.

Dorothy, or a professional driver, would then shuttle us to a park, where Sonja and I would walk for about an hour. Back at the hotel by mid-afternoon, Sonja would go into the suite's chamber

with her masseuse. Mama Henie would then cook my dinner—
which was always the same: a thick steak done very rare, a baked
potato, previously frozen green beans, and then frozen
strawberries for desert. Mama Henie then started preparing
Sonja's dinner, which consisted of about a pound of steak tartare
mixed with six raw eggs. By the time I finished my meal, Sonja
would stroll into the opulent living area of her suite, terry-clothed
head to toe and face aglow, fresh from her massage and bath. I
retreated to my small room while Sonja dined on her incredibly
weighty, gluttonous, high calorie, high protein and cholesterol
meal, and had a quick sleep and off we'd go to the arena.

After playing Indianapolis we moved to St. Louis. We stayed at
the Park Plaza Hotel, where a young unknown pianist was
playing. Sonja referred to him as Lee, and we caught the end of his
show the night before we opened. For some strange reason he
played "White Christmas," even though the holidays were a good
two months away. Unlike me, the audience had no trouble
understanding this and seemed to really enjoy it, almost like it was
his signature piece. He also played Franz Liszt's Fourteenth
Hungarian Rhapsody beautifully, and it put me right in the mind
of days with my father. Certainly there were the difficult years but
classical music always reminded me of the most pleasant days as
a child and of the many things my father taught me. Every Sunday
afternoon Dad would listen to classical music on the radio and
encourage me to do my school studies right there in the living
room with him. At times I found myself enjoying the music so
much that my homework became the accompaniment to the
concertos rather than the other way around. But I'm grateful now
since I firmly believe that without my father's interest in music I
would never have been able to make a career out of skating.
Almost by osmosis I was able to take those Sunday afternoon
feelings to the rink and allow the music to move me. It is more
than just having an ear for music—every muscle in the body needs
to be touched by each note.

As Lee went into a Gershwin medley, I thought of the time my
aunt gave me a raccoon coat to rebel against the forty below zero
weather. But I was the only one wearing this in grade school and
disliked it tremendously. So as soon as the weather improved I
took it to a pawn shop and traded it in for a clarinet. It was not a
popular move with my family, especially when I began loudly
practicing scales over and over every afternoon of the summer. It

became very clear to all of us that fondness for music and becoming a musician is about as closely related as flying in an airplane and building one. Even though my relationship with my father was now strained, I looked forward to calling him soon, just to say I was thinking about him.

Lee's encore was a boogie-woogie type number that really got the room rollicking and made me think this young man might have a pretty good career ahead of him. That night the three of us gathered for a post-performance supper in Sonja's suite. Lee spoke of his joy in playing these hotels in smaller cities such as St. Louis. He had just spent seven months in intimidating downtown Chicago at the Palmer House, and instantly the subject of gangsters came up. Before that run he was playing at The Last Frontier in Las Vegas. That's where it all began, his career took off, and so did his disdain for danger. Lee had been in a comfortable run at The Last Frontier when a gentleman abruptly tapped him on the shoulder with an offer to play at his hotel for double the two thousand dollars he was to receive from the Frontier. Lee thought the man was just a talker—how often are deals made while just walking through the casino? So he stepped up his pace and escaped into the elevator. The next night the same incident occurred, but this time Lee happened to be walking with his manager. Immediately, the manager responded with, "Well, hello Mr. Siegel."

"Yeah that's right, but call me Bugsy. Look, I want your piano man to open at my hotel, the Flamingo, okay? I'll double his salary from this sorry hotel. We've got nothing but the best right now. Jimmy Durante's and Xavier Cugat's orchestra are drawing people in from all over, but I want your piano man." As Lee relayed the story to Sonja, he explained how he agonized over the decision. He felt loyal to The Last Frontier for taking a chance on an unknown and didn't want to leave his friends there. But this offer from Bugsy Siegel was indeed a lot of money. At the same time, Lee felt it was dirty money. Before its opening on Christmas of 1946, Bugsy, a well-known Hell's Kitchen mobster, put six million dollars of the mob's money into the Flamingo, or the Pink Palace as it was known to the insiders. Durante and Cugat in the main showroom were an incredible draw but Lee simply could not make the decision. In June 1947 the offer doubled once again but by this time someone had caught up to Bugsy and his shady dealings. He was found dead with three bullets in his skull. Lee finished his run at the Frontier and made a dash to get out of Dodge. Chicago wasn't exactly saintly after Vegas, but he needed the work and it was his only offer. Now in St. Louis, he claimed to be comfortably happy and was thrilled with his new publicist who somehow managed to get people to pronounce his name right. "Sonja, you remember when we met in Vegas and people still called me 'Libber-*ace*?' Well, now my fans finally know me as Liberace, and that makes my mom back in Milwaukee very happy."

It became customary to meet with Sonja for a post performance supper either with friends who might be in town, such as Liberace, or just to go over notes on the night's show. Also customary was my escort service once again to see that Sonja had safely gotten to her room. I would drop her off and then head down the hall to my own room. Did my job. Played the game. But this one evening Sonja insisted I come in with her because she wanted "to discuss something in private." Certainly Sonja. She dashed into her bedroom. As I waited for her in the sitting room of her suite, I snickered to myself when I thought she could have easily mutilated that sentence with her fine English by saying she wanted to discuss her privates. But gratefully, her request had come out perfectly and clearly so I was happy to oblige. However, minutes later, out came Sonja in nothing more than a very flimsy gossamer negligee! Without any preamble she sat in my lap and stated, "This is the night, Michael. You have no more excuses." Measuring my words, I delicately explained that I was newly married, a father, and a Catholic who believed in his faith. But Sonja would have none of it and proceeded to have her way. I instantly lifted her off my lap and headed for the door. As I did so she ran past me, losing the negligee in a flurry, turned her back to the double doors, and dramatically stretched out her bare arms. "I am blocking the way, Michael, I will not have you get out, yah?" No, Sonja, I thought as I picked her up and carried her into the bedroom, where I unceremoniously dumped her on the bed. I had my way all right, straight to the door as Sonja ran after me pleading and screaming in Norwegian, English, and maybe a couple other languages too. It was hard to tell since her voice became more and more muffled as the elevator descended.

Immediately, I called Norah and without explanation told her to pack up the children and get here as fast as possible. Norah quickly organized and arranged for the train ride to St. Louis. Our business manager, Don, who happened to be the brother of my old friend from *They Were Expendable*, Robert Montgomery, rushed Norah to the Los Angeles train station. Missing it by seconds, they decided to race the train to its next stop in Indio, about three hours away. I'm sure that portion of the trip felt longer than the rest of the way to St. Louis.

The remainder of the St. Louis run was unremarkable as Sonja and I carefully navigated our way back to mutual respect. Even on the night that Sonja had zipper trouble she was determined to handle it with aplomb. We had entered the ice from opposite sides of the stage to meet in the middle in a dance position spin. But as soon as I put my hand on her back I realized the zipper of her costume, which ran from her shoulders to the lower back, was wide open. Although it was still hooked at the top, I asked as I held her in front of me for our pair spread eagles if she'd like to go off the ice or have me inconspicuously help her zip it up. With gritted teeth Sonja said, "Well now look who's calling the cake good." Must be a Norwegian phrase that loses something in the translation. Anyway, without missing a beat, Sonja skated into our side by side sit spins and apparently pulled her zipper up while spinning in synch with me and the music. It was a tribute to her ability and professionalism—she merely gave me a peculiar grin, and not another word was spoken.

The show was doing tremendous business and it was especially wonderful to have my family there with me. Even our opening on Christmas Day in frigid Chicago was no match for the warmth of our love. As Norah, the kids, and I strolled down Michigan Avenue, the arctic-like wind hurling off of Lake Michigan seemed to circumvent our every step. Unfortunately for Sonja the cold was only compounded by her less than warm marriage to the surly Dan Topping. He happened to be basking on a yacht in the Caribbean sunshine when he decided to place a call to his so-called loved one. Apparently, he made a habit of this call with its terse request for money, but this time his gall and ignorance even shocked Sonja. He used the short-wave radio, and anyone in the world could hear his infantile financial request from the great Sonja Henie, his wife no less. Humiliated, Sonja went ballistic, and I think there was a bit of her sour mood left over to stir that night's performance. The orchestra was set up to play beside the stage set right near the audience. As Sonja was exiting backwards after her solo number she misjudged the line and fell backwards over the low barrier and dash lights. The lighting director wisely cut off the spotlights and Sonja was sure she fell into the orchestra pit. The man she fell into asked, "Are you all right? Can I help you?" Sonja, believing she was talking to a musician retorted, "You're goddamn right you can. Get me the hell back on the ice." When she realized later that she had spoken that way to a customer, she had an usher deliver a note of apology and money to refund his tickets. But the man was good-natured and refused the money by saying that having Sonja fall in his lap made the tickets invaluable and the experience sensational.

At the top of February, we headed to New York, which was to be the highlight of the tour for Sonja. Opening night was a star-studded affair with the best seats occupied by what seemed to be only members of the upper-crust "four hundred" or elite entertainers. Topping that list was none other than Dan himself. I was happy for Sonja and hoped for the best as I could see Sonja really wanted every piece of the puzzle to fit nicely. But it was not to be. Dan Topping held a party in the press room at Madison Square Garden to honor Sonja before the show began. Dorothy Stevens nudged Sonja thirty minutes before showtime. Sonja kissed her husband, who said, "Break a leg, baby." And off she went toward backstage. Meanwhile, Dan's party continued.

When Sonja took to the ice for her first number, which was her favorite, she was aghast to see the most important box in the filled stadium, front and center, holding fifty seats, was completely void of any people whatsoever. It was Dan's box. As a tribute to his party throwing ability, yet in deference to his wife, he neglected to move the event to the box seats so prominently visible to the rest of Madison Square Garden. Sonja was so offended by his impudence, and rightly so, I almost felt I was doing the show only to act as the glue between her and the ice. She would loved to have stormed up that center aisle, made her way into the press room and honor him with a skate blade through his heart.

The only words spoken for the rest of the performance were, while struggling with her smile, she uttered, "Your goddamn pants are open!" As quickly and unobtrusively as possible I checked my zipper, but everything was okay. I then realized she must have said "fans." Sonja was particular about drafts and never wanted to skate while the massive exhaust fans were blowing to dissipate the cigarette smoke. Communicating this irrationality to the building managers was not always easy. But then communicating some of the simplest things with this Norwegian flicka wasn't necessarily a slice of strudel either. Sonja carried on with her usual sang-froid, for she would never let her audiences know of the deep hurt that skated with her every step that night. At intermission as the new ice machine called the Zamboni took to the ice, there was a firm knock on my dressing room door. It was Dorothy Stevens. "Sonja wants you to know, whether Mr. Topping joins us or not, our plans for the rest of the evening will not change." Yes, she was indeed imperturbable.

After the show Norah and I joined Sonja and a few others at the Versailles to catch French superstar Edith Piaf's late show. Sure enough, Dan was missing at this event also. There was a strong connection between Piaf and Sonja, even though they really did not know each other very well. Born in the same year, they both became stars by the outbreak of World War II. Like Sonja, Piaf was just a little slip of a woman. In fact, her real surname was Gassion but a cabaret owner heard the little girl singing and nicknamed her "Piaf," French for "little sparrow." What these women lacked in stature they certainly made up for with gumption. Piaf was famous for her song "Non, Je Ne Regrette Rien." And that is exactly how she lived her life: "No, I regret nothing." Both women were determined and went after just what they wanted, be it career or love life, they never wavered and never backed down. They proved their capacity for survival as incredibly both the little sparrow and the little flicka were faced with accusations of collaborating with the Germans. Piaf left her homeland and opened at Carnegie Hall to standing ovations in 1947. This was my first time seeing her sing live, and as I listened I was instantly struck by the sentiment in her voice and lyrics. Even though most of her lyrics were in French, I could count on Norah to translate the dramatic salient points. She was indeed eloquent, but her powerful voice expressed torment and anguish all in the name of love. On this particular night, Sonja was drawn to her like a simpatico spurned lover.

As Piaf sang her signature song, "La Vie En Rose," I glanced at Sonja. She was so engrossed from the very first phrase, "Hold me close, hold me fast, the magic spell you cast." Sonja's heavy heart and woeful eyes were the exact reflection of Piaf's who sang with such intense yearning. I held Norah's hand tighter and prayed that Sonja's destiny would bring her a love as deep as ours. "And when you speak angels sing from above, everyday words seem to turn into love songs, give your heart and soul to me, and everyday will always be la vie en rose." Miss Edith Piaf bowed to her enthralled audience. Sonja was stoic, almost as though she had reached down deep for a renewed vigor, perhaps a promise to herself once again that no man would stifle her spirit. I overheard her manager suggest to Sonja that she skate to "La Vie En Rose." Sonja shook her head while still watching Miss Piaf, "No, no, that is Edith's legacy, her strength." Sonja finished the rest of her brandy, stood up clapping, then came over to me and whispered in my ear, "Michael, maybe it is not too late for you and me. Tomorrow I will call the lawyer to start divorce papers." Yes Sonja had slipped away for a moment, but she was definitely back to her old self, and that was okay by me. I stood to help Norah with her coat while giving a tender little kiss to the nape of her neck.

Sonja bragged to me about her ability to seduce these men in order to get what she wanted from them. Many of these men were known to be womanizers themselves—Tyrone Power and others she appeared with. She made it clear to me that she wanted me sexually, and since I did not succumb she wanted to show me how many other famous men had taken their pleasure with her. Sonja's contribution to me personally was so large and comprehensive that I have the greatest gratitude for her. She created the ice show business, which gave me the income to help my family, the continued use of ice skating which undoubtedly saved my health, a wife and family, and the Hollywood acting opportunity. It was while traveling with Sonja's show when we had a month to get to know each town that I realized the need for easier, cheaper, and more accessible ice skating instruction. This gave me the idea for an ice skating school on the order of the Fred Astaire and Arthur Murray Schools of Dance. This idea proved successful and became my main source of livelihood. So I can even give Sonja credit for giving me the opportunity of developing that business, which I chose to do in Chicago because our show and Sonja were so popular and well-known there, and I felt it was the family-type of town that the skating school would need. More on that later.

We finished the tour in March after moving from New York to Detroit, another Wirtz-owned arena. We then returned to Hollywood to start on the movie, which was called *The Countess of Monte Cristo*. Sonja was not satisfied with the first director, so he was fired and a new, young director took over. His name was Fred de Cordova, and he became famous later as the director of *The Tonight Show* with Johnny Carson for a number of years. We did the skating numbers at the Ice Palace in Westwood, and the studio shots at Universal Studios. It all seemed to go normally, with no incidents except another amusing run-in between Sonja and me on our personal relationship.

The World Figure Skating Championships were being held in Colorado Springs in March during our shooting the film. Sonja wanted to go to see the new young U.S. champion, Dick Button, so she arranged a for few days off and hired a private plane to fly the two of us to Colorado Springs. She had arranged rooms for us at the Broadmoor Hotel, where the competition was being held. When we arrived at the hotel with the two pilots, she asked me to go in and register while she watched the luggage. At the desk I saw that she had reserved a suite for herself and me to share, with another room elsewhere for the pilots. I said there had been a mistake, that the other room was for me, and the pilots were to share the suite with Sonja. Well , when we got in and she realized what I had done, she used every word in her Norwegian and English vocabulary to tell the hotel management what she thought of them. The accommodations were changed, but at least I had a separate bedroom in the suite.

When the film was finished and distributed, I was asked to go on a publicity tour with it into Canada since I was still at that time a Canadian. The first stop was the Odeon Theater in downtown Toronto. I had thought the publicity people would have prepared copy for me to deliver, but when the time came for me to go on, they just pushed me onto the stage and told me to tell how I got the part and my career, et cetera. So I went out and faced a full house. I started to tell them how I got my MGM acting contract and had appeared in a number of small parts in films. But this was the first time I had gotten the girl in the end. There was a short silence, then someone started to laugh. Others followed, and soon the whole audience was laughing. I did not know why. I did not know what I had said that they thought so funny. I meant, of course, the end of the story, but they had construed it to mean another "end." I soon changed that line!

I returned to rehearsals in Westwood in the Fall for the new, 1948–1949 tour. Sonja was interested in another man, Winthrop Gardner, another impecunious New York socialite whom she later married. But she did not stop trying to persuade me to become more intimate with her. Even after she married Winnie she persisted until after the end of the tour in 1950.

The tour ended in Detroit in March, and many of the cast drove cars out to the coast since no cars were assembled out there and they were more expensive. I had offered to drive a car out for a friend of ours, John Richardson. I asked two girls in the show who lived on the coast to come with me and help with the driving because Norah expected our third child momentarily, so I intended to drive right through, nonstop. I made a deal with Norah that I would call collect from every gas station we stopped at, but if everything was okay, she would not accept the call. At the first stop we made, just outside Detroit, I placed the call and heard the operator ask her if she would accept the call. Norah hemmed and hawed for a minute then finally said she would accept it; I panicked cause I thought this meant she was having the baby! But she said no, everything was okay, but she just couldn't say no to me! Calls were expensive in those days, so for the rest of the trip she refused except when we got to Phoenix. One of the girls did not drive because she could not drive a stick shift, so that meant the other girl and I did all the driving for two thousand miles, around the clock. There were no freeways, and Route 66 was mostly two lane and poorly marked. Each state had different signing and road striping, so night driving was tiring and tricky. When we pulled into Phoenix late at night, I decided we just had to stop for rest. We could find only one motel room with two beds, so I said we'd take it. I told the girls to use one bed while I went for gas and my call to Norah. But there was no answer on our phone! She must have gone to the hospital. I rushed back to the room, woke up the girls, and said we had to keep going. We arrived in Los Angeles the next morning, and Norah was at home feeling fine. She had gone for a walk the night before when I called. Our new baby, Ann, arrived a week later, 15 March, and made my next decision very difficult and made my future work with Sonja difficult too. Something happened that really changed her feelings toward me.

Sonja, Hollywood Ice Revue in "Countess of Monte Cristo"

THE WAY WE WERE

By Jim Bowman

Sonja Henie and Michael Kirby at the Chicago Stadium in the 1950 edition of the Hollywood Ice Revue.

When Sonja Henie's flashing blades added glitter to Chicago's Christmas

Figure skater Sonja Henie was a Christmastime institution in Chicago from the late 1930s through the early '50s, headlining her Hollywood Ice Revue at the Chicago Stadium and opening the way for the ice show as we know it today.

Henie won her first world's championship figure-skating title in 1927 when she was only 14. Just nine years later she had become the biggest female box-office attraction in sports history. In her native Norway she was a national heroine—the smiling, blue-eyed, blond who started skating at the age of eight and only four years later, in 1924, placed eighth in Olympic competition. Henie won her first of three Olympic gold medals in 1928.

She turned professional in 1936 after almost 10 years of undefeated amateur competition. In her first six weeks as a pro Henie made 18 personal appearances and a movie and earned $300,000. Hollywood producer Darryl Zanuck had offered her $10,000 for the film. She held out for $100,000.

Soon Henie was on the road with her Hollywood Ice Revue, produced and promoted by Chicagoan Arthur Wirtz, who ran the Chicago Stadium.

The Stadium was transformed into an "icy wonderland" for the revue's first Christmas-night opening in 1937. The lovely Sonja and scores of dancers who had been taught to skate performed a "Babes in Toyland" routine to the light-opera refrains of Victor Herbert. The milk-white Stadium ice was surrounded by snow banks which glistened under rose, gold, green, and blue lighting. Henie appeared in other numbers as a Norwegian folk dancer, Suzie-Q, and a waltz queen, then skated to Russian, Cuban, and German melodies.

Henie's public image was sweetness personified but she was a hard-driving businesswoman who could be tough. Referring to a Stadium ice show presented in February of 1937, Henie drew a distinction between her skating and the "acrobatic" performance of the lesser-known but locally popular Superior, Wisconsin, woman, Bess Ehrhardt, who had gotten 10 encores to Henie's four. Expressing contempt for "splits and things," which she thought had no place on the ice, Henie observed: "You might as well compare [ballet dancer] Anna Pavlova's dancing to that of someone in a circus."

In 1939, the revue's third year at the Stadium, the show opened on Christmas Eve. Henie played a doll atop a candy box in a candy-store number that featured other skaters as orange, lemon, and raspberry pigs, Peter Pan, Puss in Boots, Donald Duck, Easter Rabbit, and other characters. Henie starred in a 20-minute performance from the ballet "Les Sylphides" and dance-skated the rhumba, conga, and tango. The show's finale was called "Somewhere Over the Rainbow."

Henie's last Chicago appearance was in 1953 at the International Amphitheatre. She retired from skating in the mid-'50s. In 1967 Henie married Nils Onstad, a millionaire Norwegian shipowner. Two previous marriages, to American millionaires, had ended in divorce.

She died of leukemia in 1969 at the age of 57.

IT'S SONJA AGAIN!

Here are further pictures from the comedy "The Countess of Monte Cristo", the film in which the delightful Sonja Henie returns to the screen. As mentioned in a previous issue of *Stage and Cinema*, the story concerns two barmaids determined to spend "just three days" of luxury as a fake countess and her maid in an exclusive hotel.

Olga San Juan—who impersonates a lady's maid—is not quite so convinced as the fair Sonja that this is a good idea; nevertheless she finds herself involved, and with Sonja's parting advice, "just remember to keep your nose up and your voice down", she sets about a job which she feels certain will end in a prison sentence.

With a stolen car, a stolen mink, and various items of stolen jewellery, the two girls see their adventure through, to the delight of theatre audiences and Michael Kirby, Sonja's skating lead and romantic interest in this film.

Dorothy Hart, Arthur Threacher and Hugh French are among the cast of this delightful Universal-International picture.

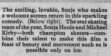

The smiling, lovable, Sonja who makes a welcome screen return in this sparkling comedy. (Below right). The star skating team of the year, Sonja Henie and Michael Kirby—both champion skaters—combine their talent to make this film a feast of beauty and movement such as is possible only on ice.

Olga San Juan goes brunnette for her role of Jenny, barmaid-cum-lady's-maid, in this hilarious comedy film.

SONJA HEINE,
Condesa de MONTECRISTO

SONJA HENIE
& MICHAEL KIRBY
IN
ntes of Monte Cristo

A scene in "Countess of Monte Cristo"

Henie, currently being
in "The Countess Of
e Cristo," a U-I release

A scene in "Countess of Monte Cristo"

Sonja Henie and Michael Kirby, romantic interests in this film.

ROMANCE ON ICE

HERE are further pictures from Universal-International's skating comedy-romance, "The Countess of Monte Cristo", which stars Sonja Henie, and marks her return to the screen. Michael Kirby, Olga San Juan, Dorothy Hart and Arthur Treacher make important contributions to this lighthearted picture.

Sonja Henie in

De Gravin van Monte Christo

Karen en Jennie, twee serveermeisjes, krijgen een bijrolletje in een film — Karen als gravin van Mont Christo en Jennie als haar kamermeisje. Karen moet in deze scène een luxe auto voorrijden voor het Trollheimen Hotel te Oslo, en het hotel binnengaan. Maar Karen rijdt met de auto weg naar het echte Trollheimen Hotel, waar zij voorgeeft de echte gravin van Monte Christo te zijn. Ze neemt haar intrek in een luxueus appartement.

En dan beginnen de dingen te gebeuren. De ,,gravin" maakt kennis met een knappe luitenant, die zij eerst voor hotelportier aanziet; er wordt bij haar ingebroken; ze eist een schadevergoeding op, die een astronomisch veelvoud is van haar werkelijke verlies; de beide meisjes raken verstrikt in de netten van een hotelrat; het is natuurlijk de knappe luitenant, die voor het gevaar behoedt, en het eind van het liedje is, dat Karen, nu verloofd met de luitenant, triomfen viert in een door het hotel georganiseerde ijsrevue.

Sonja Henie is natuurlijk Karen, terwijl Jennie wordt gespeeld door de temperamentvolle Olga San Juan. Michael Kirby is de luitenant met de mooie uniform, terwijl Hugh French voor de hotelrat zorgde, met een grote witte bloem in zijn knoopsgat. Olga en Sonja zingen verschillende liedjes.

A scene in "Countess of Monte Cristo"

A scene in "Countess of Monte Cristo"

With Catherine Littlefield, choreographer

Kirby family at home in 1961

Kirby with Dorothy Lamour in a summer theater play

7

England 1950
Rose Marie On Ice

Since there had been no Olympics since 1936, Sonja technically held the title of Women's Olympic Champion for Figure Skating since her first win in 1928. When the games resumed in 1948, a young Canadian girl, Barbara Ann Scott, won the title. Sonja resented this and the winner very much; she felt she had a proprietary interest in the title after owning it for twenty years. In the summer of 1950, during the hiatus of the Sonja Henie show from March to September, I was asked to skate with Barbara Ann Scott in a unique ice show in London for four weeks. With a new third baby Norah could not come so we would be separated again.

The show was unique in that it was a complete musical play on ice. The dialogue and songs were done by actors out of view of the audience while we skaters said or sung them in synchronization.

The show was the musical *Rose Marie*, about a young Canadian girl and the Mounties. It was a great success in London and was held over for another four weeks. In fact it was still selling out after the eight weeks and they wanted it to be extended further, but I had my commitment to return to the Sonja show for rehearsals in September.

Sonja was so mad at me for having skated with the new champion, whom she resented so much, that she did not speak to me for two months! We worked together every day, making up new numbers for the new show, which meant we skated together, and did lifts and all the movements we had to do together, but with not a word from Sonja. If she wanted to get a message to me about the number she would address the choreographer, Catherine Littlefield, who worked with us every day, and say, "Please tell Mr. Kirby to do so and so or whatever," even though I was standing right beside her, and perhaps even with my arm still around her waist!

When I returned to New York from London, I checked in with the manager of the show, and he was aware of how mad Sonja was over my skating with Barbara Ann so he told me that I would have to take a cut in salary. I told him I wouldn't and unless I had at least the same salary as before I would be on the next plane back to London, where they wanted to extend *Rose Marie*. Within hours I had a call directly from Wirtz, who told me he had talked to Sonja and she wanted me back, so my salary would be the same—an example of what a great man Wirtz was, and I like to think, what a smart woman Sonja was.

It wasn't until opening night in Indianapolis, two months later, that she spoke directly to me by inviting me to join her for her usual supper group after the show. Nothing was ever said about the London show, even though I had agreed to go back for a reprise of it the next summer.

But Sonja had a good personal side too. Every Christmas a truckload of toys would arrive for my children from the famous toy store on Fifth Avenue in New York, F.A.O. Schwartz. She also wanted to help me in my teaching career in ice skating. Sonja's concern for me and her desire to help me, allowed me to continue teaching Ronnie Robertson while we traveled on the tour. Sonja never skated during the day until noon, and she did not want anyone else to use the ice in case they hurt it in some way before she could use it. But she allowed me to have Ronnie use it in the mornings. He would go to the arena at about six in the morning and work on his figures until ten, when I came in to train him. We worked for two hours, and then Sonja came in and I practiced with her.

I knew that a number of homosexual boys in the show thought Ronnie was an excellent prize, so I let the word out that I was responsible for him to his parents and that he was completely "off limits." However, one night the boys and Ronnie broke the rules. I arranged for him to have a room next to mine, and every night I checked on him after the show. One night in St. Louis when I did so he was not in his room. After checking around the hotel with other members of the cast, I discovered that there was a "gay" party in one of the rooms. I went up to the room and discovered Ronnie sitting in a circle in the center of the room, obviously the main attraction. I confronted the host who admitted that he had induced Ronnie to come to his room. I was so mad at him that I knocked out two of his front teeth. I paid for their replacement, but I am afraid that the effect to Ronnie's psyche was already done.

Time for a Decision

By this time, 1951, Sonja had married her second husband, Winthrop Gardner, who was to cause her downfall. Every time I was with them, while traveling or at Sonja's nightly suppers, Winnie would find some way to denigrate Arthur Wirtz and keep feeding Sonja stories about how Wirtz was exploiting *her* for his own benefit. He convinced Sonja that she did not need Wirtz and she could do it alone, with Winnie's help, of course.

I had been invited back to London for a revival of *Rose Marie* with Barbara Ann for the summer of 1951 for a set sixteen week session. We decided the whole family would go so Norah packed up the three children, M.J., Tricia, and Ann, and we went to Montreal to embark on the Canadian Pacific ocean liner *Empress of Canada*, which later became one of the first Carnival Cruise ships in Florida, for the trip to England.

We had been warned about the shortages still prevalent in England from the end of the war and the control of the socialist Labor Party under Clement Atlee, so we brought as many of the scarce items such as sugar as we could. The ship arrived in Liverpool, and we had to take a train to London. In London we took a cab from the station to our flat in Marylebone Road. However, all the handling of our luggage with the extra boxes of food had caused some damage, so that as we drove across London we noticed a thin trickle of sugar streaming onto the street from the box in the overhead luggage rack on the taxi. We were so embarrassed by this display of American arrogance that we did not ask the taxi driver to stop so we could correct the leak.

Our flat was in an old building just around the corner from Baker Street, the fictional home of Sherlock Holmes and entrance to Regent Park, which proved to be excellent for the children and the young nurse we hired to look after them. She was an eighteen year old from Australia working her way around the world. She was very good with and for the children, but she made it clear to us that she was not a servant and did nothing for us. I recall her salary was the equivalent of eighteen dollars per week.

By the summer of 1951 a decision came to head when Sonja told Wirtz that she was going to go out in her own ice show. I was still in London doing *Rose Marie on Ice* when Sonja called me to tell me this and that she wanted me to continue with her. I tried to tell her that she was making a big mistake, but she was adamant. I called Wirtz to find out his plan, and he told me the *Hollywood Ice Revue* would continue, and that he was thinking of hiring "that girl you're skating with in London." He wanted me to stay and skate with her in the *Hollywood Ice Revue*. I agreed that I would, since I always knew that I was working for Wirtz, not Sonja.

What Sonja and Winnie did not realize was that Wirtz and the other ice shows, *Ice Follies*, *Ice Capades*, and *Holiday on Ice*, had exclusive contracts with most of the arenas, which prevented other ice shows from playing in them.

Sonja was unable to book shows in those arenas, so she had to find buildings that could take a portable or temporary ice rink since they did not have their own ice surfaces. Frequently, the seating had to be rearranged or added to with temporary bleachers to accommodate the large ice surface. It was expensive and time consuming to install those portable tanks, as they are called. In addition to finding buildings that could suit her needs, Sonja, Winnie, and her brother Leif, who was managing the show, did not know how to plan bookings with the best travel arrangements, so they incurred huge costs with impractical travel arrangements. But the worst disaster occurred in Baltimore.

The Baltimore building required temporary seating. During the performance on opening night, a large portion of the stands collapsed, injuring hundreds of people. Sonja was smart enough to realize that they would be inundated with lawsuits. She immediately canceled the show and ordered her cast and crew to pack up everything and get out of town. She was right about the lawsuits and hired the top lawyer of the time, Jerry Geisler, to defend her. He was smart enough to get the blame shifted over to the city's inspection department, since they had approved the seating arrangement. That took it away from Sonja, but getting that concession resulted in tremendous legal bills for her.

Between the legal bills, unnecessary travel costs, and portable ice rink costs, Sonja was losing a great deal of her personal fortune. At one of their meetings, when it looked as if they could not make the payroll, Sonja went into her room and came back with all her jewels. She dumped them down in the middle of the meeting and asked if they would bring enough to meet the payroll. When her brother and Winnie proved to be such bad managers for example, by choosing the shows itinerary from road maps that had the size of the larger towns with larger circles, she hired Frank Zamboni, who had invented the ice resurfacing machine that bears his name, and who had managed an ice rink in Southern California, to take over. Frank called me for help because he did not know anything about managing an ice show. So Sonja's problems multiplied.

Decision to Leave

Since I had chosen to stay with Wirtz, I lost all touch with Sonja for many years, except for a crossing of our paths in a sad and poignant way that first year of the split. For some reason that can only be blamed on ego, Sonja decided to play her new show in Indianapolis at the same time that Wirtz was playing his usual dates with the new *Hollywood Ice Revue*. Sonja could not play in the usual coliseum so she had to rent a college basketball arena, which required portable ice with much smaller seating. She probably thought her name could outdraw the three new girls Wirtz had to replace her, Barbara Ann Scott, Andra McLaughlin, and Carol Lynne. Unfortunately, Sonja's ego got in the way of her common sense.

I got in the middle by a thoughtless newspaper interview. A reporter asked me to compare Sonja and Barbara Ann since I had skated with both. I tried to explain in light of the immense difference in skating in Sonja's time and Barbara Ann's. For example, I have mentioned that in winning the Canadian championship in 1942 I had a maximum of two double jumps in my program. By 1948 when Barbara Ann won she probably had six or seven double jumps. Sonja had never done one double jump. I was trying to emphasize the difference in skating technique for the different times, but unfortunately it came out as a criticism of Sonja I really did not intend. We were all staying at the same hotel, so the night the story came out in the paper as I got into my car in the hotel parking lot, Mama Henie came out of the bushes beside my car with tears streaming down her face, and said to me, "Oh Michael, how could you be so cruel to Sonja who has loved you so much?" I was stricken that I had done so much damage. I begged with Mama to forgive me, saying I was quoted all wrong, which I thought I was, but I don't think I softened Mama's feelings any. I wrote a letter of apology to Sonja but never heard from her.

During the following ten or twelve years a great deal happened to Sonja. She hit the nadir of her career and her life with the failure of her ice show and a pathetic tour of Canada with an unsuccessful producer and then a tremendous resurgence in Europe with another great producer, Morris Chalfen, who was responsible for saving and revitalizing her career and fortune. The European tour Chalfen arranged for Sonja also gave her the chance to renew friendship with an old childhood friend, Nels Onstad, who became her third husband. I'm sure it was her happiest marriage.

Since I was unable to share these times with Sonja I will let her secretary of thirty years, Dorothy Stevens, tell you about them in her own words. Following are excerpts from interviews with Dorothy. The questions have been deleted, so the subjects may seem disjointed, but the following chapter is written in her words.

8

Dorothy Stevens's Story

Her time was limited on this earth, and she knew it. The day she departed from her house in Bel Air, she went to the bar room door and looked out over the yard where the dogs were. She stood there quite a long time just silently looking over the yard with the pool, tennis courts, and Sunset Boulevard curving beyond the foot of her property. Nels, her husband, said, "Come Sonja, we must get to the airport." She turned and went to the front door and I was surprised to see there were tears in her eyes, which was unusual since Sonja never cried. When she got to the door she turned and said, "Come here, Dorothy, and say good-bye. I guess we must go." When I got there she held my hand and put her arm around me. She had never done that in all my years with her. She kissed me on the cheek and said, "Good-bye, Dorothy." She had never done that before. Then she waved and got into the car with her husband. Because of that, I think she felt she would never be back, a sort of premonition. As it turned out that was her last time there. Sonja had gone into St. John's Hospital just before Christmas 1968 for pneumonia. When she was admitted and they took all the usual tests, the blood tests showed she had leukemia. Nels was shocked. "What does this mean? Are you sure? What can we do for her?" The doctor said she would require frequent blood transfusions and she would gradually get weaker and weaker. "Unfortunately, we have no cure so the disease is terminal."

Nels asked the inevitable, "How long does she have?"

The doctor said, "Less than a year, I would say about nine months."

Nels did not believe the American doctor, so he had some blood flown to a doctor in Norway, and he confirmed the diagnosis.

Now we all discussed whether to tell her or not. Mama Henie said, "Sonja must not be told." Nels agreed, and he decided to tell her that her blood was very low and she would need transfusions, but that was all.

He told me, "Dorothy you must keep her very busy. You know how excited she is about opening the Art Center and how she likes to find good art, so you must stay with her and help her so she does not tire too much." So she believed she was anemic and I heard her tell her friends that. She passed away 12 October 1969, so the doctor was right.

She was very active right to the end. I spent the summer with her in Oslo, where she was very busy with the new Art Center they were building. We flew to France and Italy to buy art. She had transfusions frequently but seemed to take them for granted. We were at her home in Lausanne after the opening of the museum in September. It was a grand opening. The Royal Family came, as did many distinguished people from all over Europe.

Sonja had been very busy buying art. She had an eye for it. She would see some unknown artist and insist on buying his work, and she would be right. Just before we were leaving Lausanne, she had another transfusion there. Sonja said, "Dorothy fly into Paris with us and we'll have a good visit on the plane. Then you can catch the flight to Los Angeles. Nels and I are going to the Prince's party in Lisbon on Sunday and then we'll join you in Los Angeles."

I flew into Paris with them, and it was apparent she was weak and probably needed another transfusion. She did not have a doctor she liked in Paris so she told Nels, "Let's get a plane for Oslo. Helmut (her Norwegian doctor) could give me a transfusion, and I can get some things organized to send to Los Angeles." They were going to spend a few days at their Paris apartment. We landed there on Wednesday, and they were going to a large party in Portugal on Sunday. The plan was that they would fly to Oslo, where all her things were packed, and then after the party on Monday or Tuesday she would fly to Los Angeles. On Saturday they went out to dinner with a good friend in Paris, Kay Grable, Clark's widow, who had ironically become Sonja's best friend. She called me afterwards all excited because they had such a good time. She was laughing and carrying on. "Kay had just flown in from Los Angeles, and she was full of the latest gossip, so she filled me in for hours. We still expect to be home by Wednesday, so will you line up a few appointments for me?" Then she told me to call her hairdresser, Elizabeth Arden, and set up an appointment for Wednesday. She wanted a manicure and pedicure, and then to go to Beverly Hills Home and Silk and get a bunch of samples for the dressmaker, Mrs. Ericson, to make me a bunch of dresses. Then she wanted to do some grocery shopping so the house would be ready for them. Sunday morning my phone rang early, and I thought Sonja had forgotten something else she wanted me to do, but Nels came on the phone and said, "Hello, Dorothy, Sonja is dead." I couldn't believe him, but he repeated, "She is dead, get the first plane and come right over."

He hung up. I did and got there the next morning. Mr. Onstad met me at the airport himself, and he seemed in shock as though he couldn't believe it. Seeing him made me suddenly burst out into tears. He put his arm around me and comforted me, but his sister who did not particularly like Sonja, came over to us and said, "Don't cry Dorothy, she wasn't worth it."

I stayed at Sonja's home in Oslo, Landoen, the first night, but it was quite far from Nels's office in Oslo, where I would have to make all the arrangements with his secretary. So it was decided that I would move to the Grand Hotel, which is a short walk from the office. I worked with his secretary on all the preparations—the lists, the wires, and all the preparations for the service at the crematorium. It was limited so people could come by invitation only. It was very strange to be sitting there writing these invitations when the first job I had for Sonja was writing invitations to one of the many fabulous parties she gave in Hollywood. I had recently driven myself out from Iowa and needed a job, so when I saw the Ice Palace in Westwood I applied there and was given a waitressing job in the snack bar. After only a few days Sonja came in for tea and started talking to me. She told me that her secretary had just quit and she needed someone to do the invitations for a big party she was planning. I told her I was trained to be a secretary so I could do it for her. That is what she hired me to do when we first met while I was working at her ice rink in Westwood.

Nels told me what happened. When Sonja got up Sunday morning she felt very tired and had a hard time getting dressed. So he said they had better hurry and go to Oslo before they went to Portugal, since they didn't have a doctor in Paris for the transfusions. He chartered a plane, and as they boarded it Sonja said she was very tired. He suggested they have a drink to perk her up, and he had a flask of scotch. Then he said she should have a little nap, and he would wake her up before they landed. It was only about a forty-five minute flight. She put her head on his shoulder and fell asleep, and he read the paper. As they prepared to land, he started to wake her up, and there was no response. He took her hand and realized it felt lifeless. He called the pilot, who came back immediately. The pilot tried to take her pulse but found none and told Nels that she was dead. They radioed for an ambulance and a doctor, who was waiting when they landed. He came on board and pronounced her dead.

I was so busy with all the arrangements for the funeral that I did not feel any emotion at the time; not even at the service. It didn't hit me until five years later when we sold her home on Delfern Drive in Bel Air.

So the funeral reminded me of her great success, thirty-five sold-out performances at Jordahl Amphi in Oslo, where fifteen thousand people stood through the whole performance. It was an especially happy time, because we had just gone through the horrors of the tour where the stands collapsed. Sonja lost her fortune and could not get more bookings. We had to take a tour offered by a Canadian promoter, Tom Gorman, to do Canadian cities in some small arenas.

The Revival

But one man had been watching Sonja for years since she left Wirtz, and he had faith that she could do it again with the right show and bookings. That man was Morris Chalfen, the owner of *Holiday on Ice* which had a successful show in Europe. On the Canadian tour Sonja had insisted on playing a small town on the coast near the U.S. border, St. Andrews by the Sea. The arena was a Quonset hut with wooden planks for seats since it was only used for hardy hockey players and fans. But Sonja had romantic memories of this town because Franklin Roosevelt had taken her there twenty years earlier when he took her to his summer home on the island of Campobello. Chalfen found us there.

He asked for a meeting with Sonja and she agreed. She met with Chalfen while Mama and I sat in the background. He said, "Miss Henie, I have most of the finest arenas in Europe under contract for my *Holiday* tours. I would like you to come to Europe and be the star of one of those tours. You could choose your own musical numbers and my entire company would support you in every way possible. I am willing to offer you a most generous contract since I know you will be a major attraction in Europe."

"Okay," Sonja said. "What's the deal?"

"I am prepared to meet with your agents or lawyers to work out a mutually agreeable contract."

Sonja said, "I make my own deals; put it on the table."

Chalfen was somewhat taken by surprise. "Well, I did not expect to get into details of the terms today, but I am prepared to offer you a fixed salary against some percent of total revenues."

"Right away we have a problem; it will be a fixed salary plus a percentage of total gross revenues," Sonja stated emphatically. "Also, I do not want to play a number of small towns, only the major cities, with transportation and costumes provided by the show."

Chalfen realized he was not dealing with an amateur, and no skater had ever talked to him like this before. But he also realized he was not dealing with an ordinary skater; he was dealing with a world-renowned movie star who had made some serious mistakes to find herself where she was, but who still had the drawing potential his people in Europe had discovered. "Miss Henie, let me prepare a specific proposal for you and get back to you. I would like you to open in Paris in just two months."

Sonja said, "Okay, but I'll be finishing this tour in a month and returning to Los Angeles if I don't hear from you."

Just then Mama Henie stood up and went over to Chalfen with a penny in her hand. Chalfen had pronounced her name as "Hynie" which annoyed Mama. She said "Mr. Chalfen the name is Henie just like penny, you understand how to say that don't you?"

Then Sonja surprised us by asking Chalfen when he was leaving and he said not until morning so Sonja said, "Why don't we have dinner together?" She had obviously taken a liking to him. He did not seem offended that she had come on so toughly with him instead of appearing grateful for the opportunity he was offering her. She explained after he left that that was the only way to deal with those producers, and she turned out to be right. They had a very successful and pleasant relationship and agreed to get together the next day. Sonja invited him for a drink, and we all went out to dinner together. The only thing available in the town was lobster, so that is what we all had. I could tell Sonja liked Chalfen, and later she told her mother she did and she thought she could trust him. Their association proved to be very successful, and they got along very well.

He convinced her not only to come to Europe but to play Norway, which she was very apprehensive about. At first Sonja was adamant. "I will not subject myself to the abuse I know I will get in Norway for my time with Hitler before the war and the accusations that I did nothing for the Norwegian war effort—which was totally false." She had been accused of throwing lavish parties in Hollywood when the Norwegian people were starving under Hitler. Chalfen said he had people in Norway, including many from the media who claimed that was not true. He convinced her to perform and offered her a percentage deal that was greatly to her advantage.

We went to Europe and played Paris, which was very successful, especially because Sonja loves Paris and has an apartment there. Then we played London during the Coronation so it was crowded and we had a very good run. She enjoyed a tremendous reception in Berlin because they remembered how she trained there before the war. They loved Sonja, and it was very emotional.

Sonja was very nervous about moving to Oslo, but Chalfen assured her that he had all his people checking there and they had nothing to fear. He was right—we had a very successful engagement, and Sonja was able to recoup most of her fortune.

After Oslo we played Stockholm—another great successful run. The show was scheduled for France, but Sonja did not want to play small towns, so she made a deal with Chalfen to let her return to the States.

All through her European run she was spending a lot of time with a friend from Norway, Kjell Holm, who remained a friend for all her life, but no romance seemed to be the result. She also renewed a childhood friendship with Nels, who had been a friend of her brother Lief but who was now only interested in Sonja. He had made a fortune in the shipping business, which was very big in Norway.

In 1955 we went to New York and played a date at the Roxy Theater, a grand old theater with a beautiful stage and setting for Sonja. We played there through March 1956, and then Sonja got the idea from Chalfen to play South America. A tour of *Holiday on Ice* had been very successful down there. Before leaving for South America, Sonja called me late one night and told me to come up to her suite with my boyfriend, Ken Stevens, who was the master of ceremonies and did all the announcing and live singing during the show. We went to her room, and she announced, "Dorothy I am sending you down now to South America to begin making arrangements for hotels, banks, transportation, et cetera."

I said, "Oh, Sonja, please send someone else. Ken and I are planning to get married soon."

She flew into a rage. "You are not getting married. You are married to my work, and you must stay exclusively with me. I want you and Ken separated, and he will remain here with the show." We were devastated since we both needed the jobs and we would lose them if we refused Sonja. So I had to go ahead, knowing that we would be together when the show played in South America.

Our first show date was in Caracas. It was very successful, and then we flew to Rio. Sonja had met Nels during the European tour and a romance had definitely sprung up. He was constantly calling her. Sonja was discouraged with the show because she was feeling her age. She was in her forties which was old for that kind of athlete and performer. She began to drink heavily on this tour, and it was pathetic. Her performances became worse and worse, and she became suicidal, threatening to jump out the window. We could not leave her alone. Mama or Carrie, her cook and good friend, or I, would be with her twenty-four hours a day. Finally, she decided she had to stop skating and made a deal with Chalfen to leave the show. Nels had been urging her to come up to New York and marry him, so that is what she decided to do.

I must say that Nels gave her a new lease on life. I had to stay in South America and stop in Caracas to pick up some money we had put in a bank there. I missed the flight to New York because the plane just did not show up, but I was able to meet them in Miami, where they went for their wedding breakfast.

She was always interested in art, but Nels really got her more so. She became better than he was at picking good artists. I felt that if it had not been for him and his efforts to interest Sonja in art, I would wonder how her life would have turned out.

As I saw Sonja reach the heights of happiness with her marriage to Nels Onstad after the depths of despair in South America, I was reminded of the many times the pendulum of happiness had swung back and forth for her.

Within a year after she left Wirtz to go out on her own we were broke. She had lost most of her fortune, and we needed help to keep going. Selling her jewels would not solve the problem. I remembered that she had an insurance policy that was probably worth a great deal. She swallowed her pride to call Wirtz about it and confess that she needed cash. He came through not only on the insurance, but also by selling some of the property he had bought for her over the years. That kept us going for another year. I remember driving with Wirtz in Chicago and passing an old, large hotel on the west side. Wirtz said, "Sonja you own that building."

Her only response was to say, "Oh, it's so crummy looking. Can't we get something more attractive?"

Wirtz said, "Sonja there is nothing that is more attractive than making money and this one makes much more money than your so-called 'attractive' buildings." When we were in such a financial bind, Wirtz's investments really saved the day for us.

Her constant fighting with Leif, her brother, and the way she turned on her mother as she was dying came from a side of Sonja that bothered me, because it seemed so out of character with so much of the good side of her. The drinking towards the end of her skating career was undoubtedly the main cause of much of those problems.

Leif was a leech on her life, as her two previous husbands had been, and that was enough to bother her. She had bought property in Oceanside, California, and asked Leif to manage it so he would have something to do out of the house. When he thought she had given it to him and it was solely his, she resented his lack of gratitude, and it led to legal battles between them. The property is still called The Henie Hills. One of the last things her mother said to me as she was dying in Sonja's house, was, "Try and get Leif and Sonja together again."

But her treatment of her mother at the end was simply unfathomable. Mama had a number of strokes and was in and out of the hospital, and Sonja resented the expense of the hospital bills. Her mother had been Sonja's slave all her life, so to be treated like this was something I could not understand. When her mother had her most serious stroke, Sonja was in Europe but not working. I called her and had to try three of her houses before I could find her. She did not want to come home, but I begged her to and told her that if she did not her mother would be dead. She finally agreed to come home. When we met her at the airport she was drunk from the flight, and Leif was with me so they fought all the way home. She continued to drink all throughout the night and got mad at the nurse for giving her mother shots that might prolong her life. She actually fought with the nurse and tried to throw her over the balcony.

Mama passed away in the afternoon, and the nurse came to me to tell Sonja. I did so and all she said was to go in and get all her jewelry, including whatever she was wearing, before Leif came over. So I had to take the rings off her body and clean out her jewelry drawer. It was very sad.

Somehow I forgave her for the harm she did me. She fought my marriage to Ken with every trick she could use. She sent me to Cuba to see about the show down there. After the show had a successful run, the manager she had hired fired me and said he was not going to pay my way home. Sonja did nothing about it.

As I went through the preparations for the funeral service and was busy with all the details that needed attention, I thought of many of these things about our relationship, but strangely enough I did so without any emotion. After the funeral I had to meet with lawyers from all the places Sonja had property and business dealings. Nels knew very little about the details of Sonja's businesses, so they had to pick my brain and memory for the two or three months it took to pull the estate together.

Sonja's entire estate went to the Art Center. She did not leave anything to any person. No one was mentioned in her will. Nels was given the right to live in her houses until they were sold, but he soon remarried and moved in with a new wife—which I knew would upset Sonja. I feel to this day that Sonja's will was not carried out as she wanted. In exchange for giving everything to the Art Center, Sonja wanted her jewelry to be on display in glass displays. That was never done, and when I mentioned it to Nels he said it was impossible because of the expense for security. Yet I saw much of it on his new wife and his daughter.

On another personal matter, Sonja had told me that if anything happened to her there was a manila envelope in the safe that was to be mine. When I got back after the funeral, although I knew the combination to the safe, I felt it would be improper for me to open it before Nels got back. He came in December and I told him about the envelope in the safe. We went to the safe and found a large brown envelope with fifty thousand dollars in large bills in it. Nels counted it out and then said that my name was not on it so it could not be considered for me. So he decided to give me two thousand of the fifty thousand for my lifetime of work for Sonja. At the time he was building a ship in Japan for fifty million dollars.

And yet the surprising thing was that although my job was closing out Sonja's estate, I really worked for Nels for four more years. I was having a Christmas Eve drink with him in 1969 when he had his first heart attack. I did not like his new marriage and wife so soon after Sonja's death, but I knew he always had other women around even when Sonja was here and took many of them to Norway with him. In 1974 I had to hurry and close up the house on Delfern because I was taking a group of fifty of his friends and business associates to Japan for the launching of his new tanker.

As I mentioned, any emotion about the loss of Sonja did not hit me until five years after her death when I was finally clearing up all her matters. The Delfern Drive house was sold in 1974—five years after her death. I was cleaning it out to be sure it was all right for the new owners. I was leaving the next morning to take a group of Nels's friends to Japan.

I arranged for the furniture to be shipped to where he wanted, for new homes for the dogs, and for all the other details of winding things up. I ran through the house to be sure no water was running or any lights had been left on, et cetera, and I went out the front door and locked it. Then something hit me! I think the entire thirty-one years I had been involved with Sonja somehow came home to me. I thought, "I will never go through that door again." My knees buckled, and I sat on the step and cried uncontrollably.

The Bel Air patrol came by to check the property, and he knew me so he got out of his car to see what was wrong. I tried to explain to him, but all I could do was cry. He said he'd get me some coffee and he did, and soon I got control of myself and was able to drive home.

The Sonja Mystique

I am very appreciative of all the time Dorothy gave to telling her story of Sonja and their life together. Dorothy's comments about Sonja show a very emotional and mercurial person concerning people with whom she had to work. Her possessiveness of people seemed to cause her to have a love-hate relationship with them, including and especially with Dorothy Stevens. Her attitude and reactions with men further indicate an inability to function normally. She tried to dominate each man and when they succumbed she lost interest in them and usually abandoned them. She chose her first two husbands because she thought they would bring her into the high social circle of New York's famous four hundred families, but neither of them did.

My theory is that she had a strong relationship with her father, and no man could replace him in her heart or feelings. She loved children and doted on Leif's three when they were young. She was loving and generous with my three children too. But this was the same family she did not want around her show. She fought Dorothy's marriage to Ken so she could have Dorothy's undivided attention and went so far as to separate them so they could not get together. She showed a conflict in herself between being strong and being insecure.

There seemed to be a dichotomy about her relationship with men. She was strong and determined, even superior, with the men from whom she wanted something, particularly for her career; but with men she wanted and needed for herself, she seemed insecure and unsure as to how she should handle them. This was another example of the dichotomy of strength and insecurity which seemed to dominate her life. Dorothy says she was aware of many differences between Sonja and Nels, particularly whether the museum would be the "Onstad-Henie" or the, "Henie-Onstad," which it ended up being. But at every point in the arguments when Nels said, "Enough," that was it, and Sonja backed down. He was in the second category of men—the one that Sonja needed.

A statement she made to me once about children has some serious psychological meaning. She said, "I have never met the man who is good enough to father my child." What do you make of that?

9

The End of a Decade

I did not have any personal contact with Sonja from our split in 1951, until one night in 1967 when she was the first person elected to the Ice Skating Hall of Fame. Even that occasion had an aura of poignancy about it.

Sonja had been unanimously elected as the first person to the Ice Skating Hall of Fame. By coincidence I was president of the Ice Skating Institute. Having been her partner, I was asked to bring her to the banquet, which was at a hotel in Los Angeles not far from her home. She graciously accepted so Norah and I arranged to pick her up. She invited us in for a drink and showed us much of her art, which she was preparing to donate to the museum in Oslo she and her husband were building. She also gave a gracious and pleasant acceptance speech a the awards dinner.

When we drove her home, however, her house was in complete darkness and all locked up. She did not have a key. We tried all the doors and windows, and the doorbell did not seem to wake her husband, whom she said must be there. We ended up waking him by throwing rocks at his bedroom window! Sonja invited us in for a nightcap, but we thought it would be discreet to withdraw. She invited me to skate with her as she practiced every day at Pickwick Ice Arena in Burbank. I made a date to meet her there, and we had a pleasant skate together. Neither of us, however, could do the things we used to do, she was about fifty at the time. That was the last time I ever saw her. Many times since then, and especially after she died in 1969, I have thought of how much she contributed to the world, and especially to me. She was a mixed-up person in many ways, but her good far outweighed her bad.

Sonja obviously pioneered the concept of ice skating, specifically freestyle figure skating, as an entertainment and artform, but it was not until the advent of television to this entertainment that it really took off in the public eye. Four people are responsible for that: Peggy Fleming, with her flawless performance in the 1968 Olympics in Grenoble France; Dorothy Hamil, who won a gold medal in the Olympics in Innsbruck in 1976; Scott Hamilton, 1984 Sarajevo, (who has become one of the most imaginative and talented producers and performers in the skating business); and the indefatigable Dick Button, the 1948 Olympic champion who struggled to bring figure skating to the public on television. Dick scrounged and begged to get figure skating on *Wide World of Sports*, and through persistence he succeeded.

Ironically, Sonja had resisted television. She felt that without color, which it did not have yet, she would be at a disadvantage in showing herself and her show; also, the clarity and scope of the cameras did not have the quality they have today. Sonja was inconsistent with this position because of the dozen or so movies she made only one, *It's a Pleasure*, was in color. And it wasn't one of her more successful ones.

Today, thanks to the effect of television and the immense growth helped and promoted by the Ice Skating Institute—which has provided so much help to investors and entrepreneurs to encourage the growth of ice facilities—skating is at the highest level it has ever been. Many latter-day stars have contributed to this growth, including and especially Hamilton and Brian Boitano. These three men, Dick, Scott, and Brian, have made men the dominant force in skating, whereas in Sonja's day (and mine, too, unfortunately) it was strictly a women's activity and the men were secondary.

Back to My Life

It is obvious that this decade was dominated by my association with Sonja Henie from 1947 to 1951, but her influence on the skating world on which I depended for my livelihood and creativity permeated far beyond our personal or business relationships.

During this decade there were other far more important events happening in our lives. Five of our eight children were born between 1946 and 1954; Michael John (M.J.), Mary Patricia (Tricia), Ann, Catherine Norah (Cathy), and Terrence Joseph (Terry), who left this world after only thirty years.

The period from 1951 when Sonja split until we opened our new skating business in 1953 was a very traumatic one for me. I missed Sonja, and although I had been skating for two summers in England with Barbara Ann Scott, I found the year-round transition of working with her both during the summer in England and the rest of the year with Hollywood Ice Revue to be very difficult. Barbara Ann had no driving force in the show as Sonja had; she was more interested in her personal life and resented having to perform. At one point she told me she felt like a mechanical doll: "They just wind me up, and I go through the motions of skating." She made extensive demands on my personal time and at the same time Wirtz was urging me to help her make the transition and replace Sonja for the success of his show. At the close of Wirtz's show in March 1952, Barbara Ann was asked to do a tour of six or eight towns in Canada. She asked me to come to skate with her. It was for very good money and I couldn't refuse, but I was beginning to have serious misgivings about spending so much time away from my family. We were expecting our fourth child in the fall of 1952, and I felt I was missing so much with my family. Norah came with me to England for the summer of 1951, and we took a flat in London and had a pleasant summer. Tricia was only three but began speaking with an English accent by the end of the summer.

During the summers of 1952 and 1953 I took a job teaching skating at the rink at Michigan State University in East Lansing. It was giving private lessons only and not what I wanted to do with teaching. It was good pay but very tiring and difficult. I was in my skates from before six in the morning to seven or eight at night. My feet were killing me by halfway through the day. The gratification was provided by the many wonderful pupils I had, many of whom went on to major accomplishments in skating, including two pupils who became presidents of the United States Figure Skating Association (USFSA).

By the end of the tour in Spring 1953, I arranged with Wirtz to leave since I had decided to try my skating instruction program in Chicago. When we returned from England in the fall of 1951, we stayed in Chicago at a hotel on the north side while we looked for an apartment. We found one in Oak Park and moved in the Fall while I rehearsed the new show at the Chicago Stadium. Our son M.J. started kindergarten, and we began to feel like we were settling down. We were able to buy a house from a friend who worked for Wirtz as general manager of his hockey team, the Chicago Black Hawks. The house was a few doors from an excellent parish school, which all our children attended, St. Luke's in River Forest. They could walk half a block to school without crossing a street. In the spring of 1953 when I decided to stay in Chicago and start my new teaching program I first thought it should be in an existing rink, so I made a deal with the owner of a small rink in a suburb about thirty miles out of Chicago. But when I returned from Lansing in the fall he had changed his mind, and that deal fell through. I began to search the north side of Chicago near the Ice Arena, home of the Chicago Figure Skating Club for a new location. I was proven wrong for a number of reasons. This major event happened that affected and still affects the entire family. That event was the opening in 1953 of the first Michael Kirby Ice Skating School in River Forest, Illinois. Let me tell you how that came about and its meaning to us and to the skating world.

10

Michael Kirby Ice Skating Schools

I had originally thought of the skating schools as another way of teaching figure skating. When I first started looking for a location for a studio rink in which to teach, I did so near the Chicago Arena, home of the Chicago Figure Skating Club, as I imagined the studio would be an adjunct to the arena. When I was discouraged at not finding anything reasonable near the arena, a kind old lady, our next door neighbor in River Forest, Mrs. Murphy, told me about a building down the street which she thought fitted my needs. Through the cooperation of the elderly man who owned the property, I was able to get a good deal on the location of my first ice skating school in 1953. It was in River Forest, far from any ice rink. The ice surface was only thirty feet by forty feet, a long way from the official ice rink size for hockey and figure skating events, of 185 by eighty-five feet. It was the first studio-type ice surface. The reaction from the general public was a surprise to me. As the first customers began signing up for lessons, I suddenly realized that they were not all ice skaters! Many of them asked if we provided skates, which made me realize that I did not have any for them. We had sent out a brochure in early December (with all the other Christmas mail—smart!) and the response was so great that we stopped mailing before half was sent. We scheduled the opening for 23 December, our wedding anniversary, and we were swamped. I spent all the next day driving to every sport shop in Chicago to buy ice skates, at retail of course! Fortunately I knew enough about ice skates to only buy those that would support the skaters' ankles properly. Unfortunately, many skate boots were made of poor "split" leather, which was no better than paper in supporting the ankle so people who wore them thought they had "weak ankles," one of the great misconceptions that hindered the growth of skating. Another factor was skate blades that were not made of steel; the blade was made of a cheap tin alloy, which was not strong enough to retain its own shape with any heavy use. When it was put under a sharpening stone it would simply disintegrate. Now you know where the expression "cheapskate" gets its meaning. As these new customers came into the skating school, I realized a whole new system of teaching skating had to be devised. To try to teach these people what was then considered to be, and still is, elementary figure skating, would have been a terrible failure and a confirmation of why figure skating was so lacking in participants. So called "beginning" figure skating was light years out of the reach of the general public to whom the skating school appealed.

In 1953 I wrote my first book on ice skating, *Skating For Beginners*, with Barbara Ann while we worked in the *Hollywood Ice Revue*. But from what I soon learned in the skating school, it was ridiculous as instruction for real beginners.

Shortly after the skating school opened, I was visited by an old friend who had been a roommate in *Ice Follies*, Einar Jonland. He immediately saw the merits of this new approach to ice skating instruction and made a tremendous contribution to the development of the program. He thought that since I was calling it a school, I should follow the structure of the school year and sell tuition, and not lessons. He went a step further and suggested that we only sell tuition in school semesters. At the time we were selling lessons a month at a time. Einar's idea would mean selling eighteen weeks at a time. This was a revolutionary and scary thing to try to do. Fortunately it turned out to be the cornerstone of the skating school as a business. Einar and I worked well together on the growth of the business until his early death in the mid-1960s.

With this new concept of really being a school with regular semesters, and with the customers not being interested in figure skating, we had to come up with a completely different curriculum. We had a great staff of instructors who understood this new concept very well, so we worked together to develop new courses for this curriculum. Norah, Einar, a great girl (Jeanne Gross, now Mrs. Bob Couffer), Ralph and Sylvia Evans, and others worked with me on a step-by-step, simplified set of skating courses. They contributed in the most expansive and innovative way to the increasing growth and success of the school. Peter Dunfield, later a president of the P.S.A., was extremely helpful in making a study of all the major ballet companies in Europe that confirmed that they only taught in class format.

Another revaluation that occurred to me shortly after the opening of the skating school in River Forest was that private lessons were inimical with the financial success of the school. The economics were simple: a class of twenty students at about $2.50 per person generated an income of fifty dollars per hour. At that time private lessons generated about eight dollars per hour. This was driven home to me by the fact that two of my private lesson pupils had qualified for the world team in figure skating. Miggs Dean and Ronnie Robertson, whom I had been teaching for some time, qualified at the U.S. National Competition for a place on the world figure skating championship team scheduled for Oslo, Norway, in February 1954. Since I was their official instructor, I was expected to take them to the championships in Norway. Another incidence of Sonja Henie being in my life without my realizing it. Here I was participating in my first international competition in Sonja's hometown of Oslo. Some of the young skaters I met in Norway are still in touch, including Reidar Borjeson, who is now an official with the Henie-Onstad Art Center in Oslo.

Miggs made the team, although she was an alternate because the third place girl on the team, Carol Heiss, broke her leg and had to drop out. Miggs paid her own way and paid me for my time, but Ronnie could not afford to pay me for lessons and had not done so for some time. In those days there were no scholarships or sponsor funding because of the strict amateur rules, so I ended up paying Ronnie's way to Norway. His family also could not pay his way to Norway, but suddenly, the day before Ronnie was to compete, his father arrived in Oslo. I was really annoyed because they said they couldn't pay for Ronnie's trip, but now the father could afford it! My new skating school business needed all the funds I could afford for it, but I rationalized taking Ronnie to Norway thinking he would contribute to the public relations of the new business. When that proved to be so wrong, I knew that private lessons and potential world champions were not inducements for customers to the new skating school business concept, which was a completely new market plan. I then told all my private lesson pupils that private lessons would no longer be available.

We conducted numerous surveys to find out what attracted people to the school and were amazed to learn that most came for fun and pleasure; then pleasant exercise; then rhythm, timing, and coordination; and then social reasons. Those who came "to learn to ice skate" ranked fifth in motivation. After that we never used the phrase "learn to ice skate" in our advertising. The closest we came was, "Learn to enjoy the pleasure and benefits of ice skating." And it worked.

Expansion Possibilities

A few months after we opened in River Forest, I was visited by the refrigeration contractor, John Heinzelman, who had provided our refrigeration for the ice surface. He had a man with him, Paul Anderson, who owned an ice plant that sold ice blocks and cubes to businesses on the south side of Chicago. Someone had told him of the success of our skating school, so he asked for the meeting to see if I would do the same thing for him on the south side. His ice plant was idle most of the winter since people did not need to buy ice, but Heinzelman had told him that the ice plant could be used to make an ice rink. Paul Anderson asked me if I would sell him a "franchise." I didn't know what "franchise" meant, so he explained that if I helped him set up and run his new ice rink he would give me a percentage of it as a franchise fee and call it a Michael Kirby Ice Skating School. Paul and I hit it off well right away. I convinced him that a small, studio-type rink for teaching as well as the full-size outdoor rink frozen by his refrigeration would service the public skating demand. His rink and skating school opened in the fall of 1954 and was known as The #2 Michael Kirby Ice Skating School and Public Skating Rink. It too proved to be a huge success. Ironically, the Chicago Ice Arena closed and was sold to a television studio, so we were the only ice rink in Chicago, and the Figure Skating Club came to rent ice time from us. I had decided to start the first skating school in Chicago because I felt Chicago was a family oriented town, I knew a number of people from the many months we spent there with the ice show, and it was Wirtz's headquarters, so I thought I could get help from him. And I did; he was wonderful to me in many ways with the business and the cooperation of his stadium later for our ice show recitals. In fact, it was over one of these shows at the stadium that my schism with the USFSA began.

After the success of our first two skating schools, we began to look for other locations. Einar lived in Glenview, a northwest suburb of Chicago, and he thought that area was a great potential market for a skating school. We found an old, abandoned movie theater in the center of Park Ridge, another suburb in that area. We were able to make a good deal on its rent, and thanks to a young loan officer at First National Bank of Chicago, Mark Baxter, we were able to arrange the financing necessary for the remodeling. As you know, all movie theaters have a floor that slants down toward the screen to permit viewing from each row. To level that floor for the ice rink was a major expense. My memory does not confirm who came up with the idea of how to correct the problem—Einar, Heinzelman, or myself—but we ended up taking all the seats out and simply filling the entire area with sand, so there was a level from the entrance to the stage. We then laid the refrigerant pipes on the level sand and froze it solid.

The Park Ridge school opened successfully, and we celebrated by taking a train to New Orleans with friends who had been our first and best customers at the opening of our first in River Forest, John and Ruth O'Leary. On the Christmas Day after we opened, I was working in the school trying to build shelves for all the skates I had bought the day before, and deciding whether to put them up for sale or rental when a nicely dressed man came in the back door and asked for the owner. I thought he meant the owner of the property and started to tell him where to find him, but he said he wanted to meet the owner of the business. When I said I was, he asked why I was doing manual labor, so I answered the usual money restraints, et cetera. He asked a number of questions about the program and then signed up his eight children and his wife and arranged to rent the place every Saturday night for a family skating party. Needless to say, he was our best customer and remained so for many years.

The meetings with John and especially Paul were the closing highlights of this decade. Paul became godfather to our next child, the first born in the next decade, whom we called David Paul, but whom Paul Anderson insisted on calling Paul for the rest of his life. David is one of only two of our eight children who chose ice skating as a career. David won a U.S. national figure skating title in 1972 in the novice division, but it was a national title. The next year as he was training for the junior division he broke his ankle and was out of skating for a year. George Eby, our friend and my boss as the president of *Ice Capades*, realized that David's loss of a year's training seriously hampered his amateur career. He suggested that this might be the best time for David to consider a professional career—with, of course, *Ice Capades*. The company made a generous offer to David, and he became a very successful solo star of the show. During his time with the show he met the lovely girl, Holly, who became his wife. They went into teaching skating as they started a family, and today David is responsible for the management of the two most successful ice rinks in the country, the Galleria Ice Centers in Dallas and Houston.

Set for "Countess" in Sonja Henie's Ice Palace, Westwood, Los Angeles; camera on box sled in center

Michael, Dorothy, Sonja, Olga

Mama Henie, Sonja and Michael overwhelmed

Sonja And 'Mike'

There's a sparkle in the eye of Sonja Henie as she dines with her new skating partner in New York. His name is Michael Kirby, and he is under contract to MGM. Sonja's appearance at her eleventh annual ice show for the first time sees her skating with a movie star. And the gossips do say that Sonja and her new skating partner not only spend a lot of time together on the ice but go out together a great deal.

—International News Soundphoto.

THAT FIGURE OF EIGHT GIRL

by MABEL STONIER

She's Sonja Henie, of course, prettier than ever. After an overlong absence from

the screen, she's skating back with a swirl and a song in "The Countess of Monte Cristo"

WITH a skirl of skates and a swirl of skirts our favourite Norwegian star, Sonja Henie, is leaping back to the screen after an overlong absence from the studio rinks. The film in which this dimpled athlete of the ice skims back into our hearts is an amusing piece called *The Countess of Monte Cristo*, a Universal-International picture, also featuring new leading man Michael Kirby and old favourite Arthur Treacher.

Sonja's charming contralto singing voice makes its first appearance on any soundtrack in this film, and she herself cuts plenty of ice in a sort of buswoman's holiday rôle as a Norwegian film actress who also skates.

But perhaps in real life it's been rather the other way round, with Sonja as a skater who also acts, for this is her first film since way back in 1944 when we had the pleasure of watching her in *It's a Pleasure*.

Sonja first put her warm personality on ice for the benefit of picturegoers in 1936 when she lived up to the title of the delightful *One in a Million*, and then

slid gracefully from success to success with a film a year. She was plump and pretty in those days. She's prettier than ever now but not quite as plump, having neatly doffed twenty-five pounds surplus and donned instead those sleek streamlines that are so vastly becoming.

But this new look was not won through the drastic dreariness of dieting. That sort of business is against the Henie principles, which are all in favour of eating plenty and liking it—particularly when Chinese food and ice cream figure on the menu.

Sonja believes in well-balanced meals for well-balanced skaters, and also drinks a quart of orange juice a day and ditto of milk, with lots of sugar added when she feels in need of extra energy. For the achievement of the body beautiful, she puts her faith in regular exercise.

Apart from her strenuous activities on ice, she likes water in its liquid form, too—for swimming. She's won trophies for swimming, running and ski-ing, and other forms of energy expenditure include tennis and dancing,

so that she's a practiser of what she preaches about exercise.

Sonja must have been practically weaned on ice, for she's more or less skated her way up from babyhood, and was practising figures of eight at the age of eight in her home town of Oslo. A year later she won top marks in the junior competition at the Oslo Skating Club, and just to prove that this was no fluke, she won it again the following year.

Taunts The Spur

Tiring of such kid stuff, she then graduated into the adult skating class at the ripe old age of eleven by winning the Norwegian National Championship.

Shortly afterwards, her first look at the Olympic Games acted like a red rag to her ambition, and the eleven-year-old at once issued a proclamation to her family to the effect that she intended to win ten world championships and three Olympic championships. The temerity of this tot announcing her intention of achieving something which no other skater had ever attained was greeted with hoots of derision from the family.

Sonja never heard the last of it, but the good-natured teasing made her all the more determined to hit the bullseye, and the family had to swallow its discomfiture, eat its words, and generally tie itself up in apologetic knots as Sonja securely snaffled one championship after another to her flying heels.

By the time she retired undefeated from amateur competition in 1936 she had fulfilled her vow to the last trophy, having added exactly three Olympics and ten world championships to her collection, according to plan.

After that she decided to turn pro, and put on a show at New York's famous Madison Square Garden, which gave the talent spotters ideas, but not big enough ones for Miss Henie's approval. One studio gave her a test then cancelled it as part of a current economy drive. Another offered to put her in a short, but Sonja said pooh to that. It was all or nothing with her, so she rented a rink in Hollywood and put on her own show, making sure that the audience was well filled with filmic big-wigs.

Success Well Earned

Next day, Darryl Zanuck signed her up for five years, and so began the series of films starring the unusual little brown-eyed blonde who drifted and whirled across the ice like a snowflake in the wind.

In the U.S.A. particularly, Sonja has well-earned her title of Queen of the Ice, for with her films and touring ice shows, she has done more to popularize

skating there than anyone else. As a direct result of her revealing so winsomely the delights of movement on ice, scores of rinks froze into action in the States and millions of American became skate-conscious and tried to tread in the slippery Henie skateprints.

This little genius of the ice was the first to start the big ice spectacle on its swift rise to world-wide popularity.

But the Henie success is well-earned and she certainly works hard for it. During rehearsals and takes for *The Countess of Monte Cristo*, she skated altogether about 750 miles, which means that her total "skaterage" for her ten films works out at 7,500 miles. Add to that another 50,000 miles or so that she's legged it across the ice during her ten years' work in her touring show, and you get a slight idea of how to make millions of dollars the hard way.

Probably Sonja's philosophy of life has helped a lot to put her on top of the world. It's quite a simple one, which she passes on to everyone: "Don't worry. And laugh a lot. You can always find something to laugh at, if you look around."

Too true, and at least she has no need to worry about the result of her very welcome return to films.

Sonja Henie, whose films have put many names on the road to fame, has a new leading man in "The Countess of Monte Cristo"—Michael Kirby

The "Countess" thinks Michael is the doorman

1579-112

A MUSICAL ICE - TRAVAGANZA!

THE COUNTESS OF MONTE CRISTO

SONJA HENIE

with

MICHAEL KIRBY
OLGA SAN JUAN
DOROTHY HART
ARTHUR TREACHER

and

FREDDIE TRENKLER

The Countess Of Monte Cristo

Sonja Henie, the Queen of Ice Skaters, returns to the screen, after an absence of four years, in Universal - International's "The Countess Of Monte Cristo." *Left:* Sonja with Michael Kirby, her leading man in "The Countess Of Monte Cristo." *Right:* Sonja and Michael in another of the six skating numbers in the picture. Michael also skates with Sonja in her ice shows.

Below Left: Assistant Director Ronnie Rondell tucks Sonja in bed for a scene in "The Countess Of Monte Cristo." *Below:* A scene in the ice extravaganza in which Sonja, a poor barmaid, performs a Calypso number during the Christmas Festival while posing as the Countess Of Monte Cristo. Sonja is always at her best when doing intricate dance numbers on skates.

Feb. 1949

28

Kirby family at Norah's birthday party, August 1999

11

Decade Four 1956-1963

As the skating schools became more popular and well-known, we were given many opportunities to open in new locations. One was in a new family club in a suburb on the south side of Chicago, Dalton. It was a large complex with many activities. To publicize the opening we arranged with Coca-Cola and a DJ from a Chicago radio station to do a publicity tour of our locations by helicopter. The parking lot at the Dorchester Club in Dalton had not been finished or paved, so they had arranged for a large tarpaulin about forty feet square for us to land on. As we approached there was a large crowd, mostly children, circled around the tarp. On the way to land the pilot said, "I hope they have that tarp firmly secured." Just as he said that, the tarp suddenly flew up off the ground as our propwash lifted it up in front of the helicopter. When it got just above us, it was suddenly sucked back into our propeller and broke off the rotor blades. They flew away over the heads of the crowd, fortunately; if we had been a few feet lower they would have plowed right into the crowd with huge damage. When this happened, the helicopter dropped like a stone, breaking the undercarriage landing gear as well as the extended fuselage. The DJ and I were able to get out and walk away, but the pilot had a serious back injury and had to be taken care of by the medics.

We took a contract to add an ice skating school operation to another ice rink that had opened on the north side of Chicago, the Rainbo Arena. We did the same for an ice rink in a suburb of Minneapolis. And we opened a combination rink and school in a new shopping center in a small town west of Chicago, Meadowdale. At the same time we entered into franchise agreements with a couple from Toronto and a group from Cleveland.

Two of my first figure skating instructors in Winnipeg in 1938 were Robert Dench and his wife, Rosemarie Stewart. They had gone on to star in *Ice Capades*, which was formed in 1940 by a group of arena owners who saw the success of *Ice Follies* and the *Hollywood Ice Revue*. The Denches later became directors and choreographers for the show. In 1963 they decided to retire, and Bob called me and asked if I could take over his job of training the principal skaters in the show on a part-time basis. I was operating the skating schools and having the usual business growing pains, so it seemed like a pleasant diversion and source of income. I would take about one week per month, fly to the city where the show was playing, work with the skaters every day, and watch them perform at night. Most of the show stars I worked with were former national or world champions—Tommy Litz, Aja Zanova, Otto and Maria Jelinek, Lynn Finnegan, and many others. There were three separate traveling companies of *Ice Capades*, and in a couple of years the company had me fly to each one of them, so it became almost a full-time job.

It was a pleasant and rewarding job because my pupils were all champions and professionals. They appreciated the help I gave them, and despite their accomplishments they were humble enough to realize that to stay on top they still needed coaching. But by 1968 a major change occurred.

Ice Capades had been purchased by Metromedia, which felt that *Ice Capades* should get into the recreational skating business, as well as the shows. They thought this would give the shows a closer knowledge of amateur skaters coming along. It was a sort of vertical control: when the skaters depended on *Ice Capades* as they grew through the amateur ranks, they would be more inclined to join the show when they decided to become professionals. As a result *Ice Capades* bought an existing ice rink in a mall in a suburb of Los Angeles.

They soon realized that the business was more complicated than it seemed, so they came to me and asked if I would set up my skating school-type of operation in a chain of rinks they planned. I stopped working with the shows and started the skating schools in the two Chalets they then had. With their plans for expansion it became a full-time job, so in 1970 we moved to Los Angeles, and I took the job of general manager of the Chalet Division of *Ice Capades*.

We were offered an opportunity to operate a number of ice rinks in Japan so George Eby and Dick Palmer and I attended to a meeting with Mr. Tots, the owner of them and then considered to be one of the wealthiest men in the world. An interesting development ensued. I had a wonderful administrative assistant, Kathy Cole, in the *Ice Capades* office, and while we were meeting in Japan it became necessary for me to obtain some additional information from my office. We had met with the Japanese businessman in his lavish conference room, which consisted of a number of comfortable armchairs with a small individual table in front of each. While we waited for the meeting to start a few young ladies, well-dressed in white blazers and pleated red skirts, came in, bowed in front of each of us, and then knelt by our table serving tea as a Japanese ritual. Kathy Cole would bring tea into my office every day, and we would discuss events, so when I cabled her for the information I needed I added that "girls here serve tea on knees."

In her reply, after giving me the necessary information, she added, "To serve tea on knee means raise in pay for me!" Kathy and her husband Jeff live near us in the desert, and her children baby-sit when our grandchildren visit.

The *Ice Capades* opportunity seemed a practical fit with my responsibilities at the skating schools, which were not generating the revenues we needed since the bankruptcy of 1960 and 1961.

Moose Dunne, whom Mark Baxter at the bank had recommended to me, was very personable and understanding, and we got along personally, but his practical business sense was not sufficient for this type of business and he was unable to provide the necessary capital to support it. At the same time, Paul, the owner of an ice-making plant, among many other businesses, wanted me to join up with him. I was afraid that he was too dominant for me and that I would be lost in his organization, so I elected to go with Moose. With the advantage of hindsight, I now consider that the worst business decision I ever made. It was the realization after two or three years with Moose calling the shots that I was not going to realize my ambition of having a nationwide chain of ice skating schools that made me feel the *Ice Capades* offer was acceptable.

Ice Capades Chalets

It was shortly after this that fate again struck—this time led by George Eby. It was obvious that each *Ice Capades* traveling company needed its own skating coach and I could not cover them all. In his usual thoughtful and magnanimous way, George gave me a generous contract with the freedom and authority to develop more Chalets as I saw fit. He supported me in every way, and over the next ten to fifteen years we built and operated twenty Chalets all over the country and even had one franchise in Johannesburg, South Africa. My relationship with George was very pleasant and productive. Although I made many mistakes along the way, the only reprimand I can remember from George was a mild question with raised eyebrows when I had made a $200,000 mistake. I had been negotiating with a major developer for a Chalet in a proposed mall in San Antonio. The project fell through and the Chalet with it, but I had felt so confident that we had a deal that I ordered the $200,000 worth of equipment that we usually put into new location. After I reported all this to George, at the next staff meeting in his office he raised his eyebrows at me and said, "Michael are you telling me that you have ordered $200,000 worth of equipment for a Chalet that does not exist?" It was a greater rebuke than if he had yelled at me.

The first year of my new relationship with *Ice Capades* was not on a full-time basis. I felt I still had some obligations to the skating schools in Chicago, and we had some hope that we could sell them to *Ice Capades*. But this was obviously impractical for a number of reasons. We decided to move to the Los Angeles area in 1969. This was a difficult decision because I still hoped the skating schools would grow but I was also convinced that that would not happen under Moose's guidance.

An interesting sideline to this decision was that I was also negotiating with Tom Scallen, then owner of *Ice Follies*. This had some nostalgic value for us since Norah and I had started our professional careers with *Ice Follies*, and it was that show that had put us together and led to our marriage. So I was somewhat torn between the three possibilities; go with *Ice Capades* or *Ice Follies* or stay with the Michael Kirby Ice Skating Schools. I called Wirtz to ask his opinion since he had dealt with both the others and knew me and my school system. His answer to me was, "You won't go wrong with George Eby." And he was sure right. By developing twenty chalets and establishing my skating school system in them, I was accomplishing my dream of a nationwide skating school program. He gave me that satisfaction, so I forgave him for some decisions he made later in our relationship that caused me to retire early from *Ice Capades*. But we still remained good friends, and Norah and I took a number of vacation cruises with George and his charming and lovely wife, Denise. Denise introduced us to a real chalet owned by her sister in Switzerland near Lausanne. We had the pleasure of visiting there a number of times with Denise and George and a couple of times by ourselves.

12

Family Matters

When we decided to go with *Ice Capades* full time and move to Balboa Island, we may have been the proximate cause of the tragedy that happened to our son Terry a few years later. At the time of our move, Terry was just sixteen years old, a star hockey player, and the captain of his team. In his eyes our move to California would deprive him of his hockey, which was his life. He could not believe that there could be any good hockey in California. Maybe he was right—ask the L.A. Kings!

Our move to California was traumatic for Terry. In Chicago he was a well-known hockey star and the captain of his team. He felt that there was no hockey to speak of in California and so was denied his only love. On two occasions he ran away from home to return to Chicago. Both times the police picked him up and returned him to us. When Tricia, who had married Dennis Shafer and was living in our old town of River Forest, heard about this, she offered to have Terry live with them so he could return to Chicago and his hockey program. So then we gave him a ticket to Chicago and he moved in with Denny and Tricia.

Unfortunately, his freedom allowed him to develop a way of life that eventually destroyed him, and he died from a tragic accident in 1984 at age thirty. He fell or jumped off the third floor balcony while fighting with his girlfriend and suffered massive internal damage as well as a broken back. Six months in hospital fixed most of those but did not discover a small aneurysm in the brain caused by the fall. However another six months caused the aneurysm to grow and affect his brain action. The doctor said they could operate when he went to the local hospital near Balboa Island, but that there was a chance that he might end up as a vegetable. I made the most difficult decision of my life when I said to the doctor, "Let's give the good Lord twenty-four hours to see which way he goes." Terry died in a coma the next morning.

When I think of the terrible troubles Terry suffered, I wonder how much my success and fame from the skating schools, television announcing, and appearing in theatrical plays and directing debutante cotillions in Chicago, Milwaukee, and Oak Park were hollow victories at his expense. Even being elected to the Ice Skating Hall of Fame at that time may have cost me valuable time with my son.

Two momentous family happenings made us very happy during this period. Our two older daughters, Tricia and Ann, each got married. Tricia was enrolled at Loyola University in downtown Chicago as a pre-med student, which was very rare in those days. On Christmas Eve 1966, I got a call from Muriel Abbott, who produced the ice show on a small surface in the Boulevard Room of the Conrad Hilton Hotel. Her show was scheduled to reopen on the day after Christmas, and two of her key girls had called to say they would not be back after their Christmas break. So Muriel hoped I would know someone who could take their place. We were busy decorating the tree with the family when Norah and I began going over possible names of girls for Muriel. As we were doing this, Tricia suddenly spoke up and said, "What about me, Dad?" We knew Tricia had the ability, but she just didn't occur to us. So we talked and she convinced us she could do it and still continue with college, so I called Muriel and arranged for Tricia to meet her on Christmas Day. Muriel was very pleased with Tricia, and she started in the new show right after Christmas. Now I am not sure this had any bearing on the fact that Tricia married a fellow student at Loyola within the year but she did look gorgeous in her brief skating costumes in the show; certainly not the average college co-ed. So things developed at school, and she and Denny got engaged during the summer and planned an October wedding. Denny is Polish and at that time Polish jokes were popular, so poor Denny bore the brunt of much joking, especially when he offered to fix one of our phones that was malfunctioning since he worked part-time for the phone company. He was able to get it apart but not back together again, so he had to call for emergency help.

Tricia had also convinced him that I was so old fashioned that he would have to formally ask me for her hand in marriage. So Denny called to invite me to lunch for an "important discussion."

I must confess that I didn't make it very easy for Denny, which can be attested by the fact that when he was driving me back home after lunch he stopped to let me out in front of the wrong house a couple of blocks away from ours. I think I had already agreed to their betrothal, but he was still rattled. But after thirty years we still love him and praise him for all he has done for Tricia and their five children. They gave us our first grandchild, Shannon, in 1969, but we had most of the rest of our children still at home. Tommy was only eight years old, so we weren't ready for grandchildren yet. I'm afraid we dropped the ball as grandparents for those first few years.

Shortly after Tricia and Denny's wedding, one Thursday Ann and her boyfriend Jerry Staab came in and announced that they were getting married the next Saturday, two days away. We pleaded with them not to do so hastily, and I was so upset I cried. They insisted and had friends who had made all arrangements for a church and reception. Norah and I went to the church for the wedding at the insistence of our good friend Father John Fahey, who had married Tricia and Denny and had been one of their professors at Loyola. Father Fahey was one of the priests we worked with in the Pre-Cana program, and he also had Norah and I lecture to his class on marriage at Loyola—but not when Denny or Tricia were there; they got enough of it at home.

Our youngest daughter, Cathy, had started college at Marquette in Wisconsin but was able to transfer to Notre Dame when they accepted women as full-time students. In fact, she was able to graduate with the first class of women to graduate in 1974.

During 1968 and 1969 when I was beginning my transfer to the Chalet division of *Ice Capades* I was spending half of every month in California, so I had Monty Rumbold arrange for me to rent property on Balboa Island in Newport Beach. I thought it was marvelous, so when we decided to move here permanently we rented for the first year on Balboa Island. Within a year we decided that it was where we wanted to be, so we bought a duplex at 320 Coral Avenue, Balboa Island, with the Dunnes as partners since we expected it to be an investment until we could afford to move to a waterfront home. We lived there until 1988 and bought out the Dunnes a few years earlier when we got a boat, and that became our waterfront home. We are so grateful to Monty and Chuck Rumbold for giving us this opportunity for such pleasant living on Balboa Island.

Monty also introduced us to Marilyn and Les Grant who had a delightful thirty-foot Islander sailboat and introduced us to the thrill and pleasure of sailing on the Pacific Ocean. Les invited me to crew for him on the world's largest international yacht race, Newport to Ensenada, Mexico, a number of times until we got our own boat. The Grants also introduced us to Voyagers Yacht Club, where we enjoyed many interesting people and sailing lovers.

My Vietnam war experience happened by accident in December 1973. I had been asked to go back to Chicago to direct and announce the Passavant Cotillion, which was the debutante "coming out" ball for Chicago society held just before Christmas. This year it was on 22 December. My job included supervising the orchestra so that they did not cheat the hospital with overtime or provide less than contracted so it meant that I had to stay until the dance ended which was usually three in the morning, so I did not get to bed until four. Cathy was just going on her Christmas break from school, so we arranged to meet at the Chicago airport in the morning for an eight o'clock flight to Los Angeles. I left a message with the hotel operator and because of my hearing I also asked security to have someone pound on my door. I had only been able to get first-class seats because of holiday rush, so the minute we got on board they began serving wine and Bloody Marys. On my two hours sleep I had not recovered from the night before, so we flew out here in more ways than one! At LAX I gave Cathy the keys to the car, and I waited for her sitting on my luggage on the sidewalk in front of the terminal. While there a group of antiwar demonstrators came marching down the sidewalk carrying their banners and clearing everyone away. Well, I was still high enough to be outraged at this since our oldest son was in Vietnam with the Navy at that time. So I not only refused to move off the sidewalk, but I decided to disband the group all by myself. I marched right through the middle of them, pulling down all their banners and pushing some of them in the bushes. The police escorting them from the back gently put their arms around me, after I got through the whole group, and said they sympathized with me but they were required to let them demonstrate. When I went back for my luggage it had disappeared, so they got the last word.

The "coup de grace" on my reputation as a husband occurred later that day. When Cathy and I arrived home I thought I'd better have an afternoon nap to prepare myself for the fancy anniversary dinner I had scheduled with my bride. Unfortunately, when I woke up it was the next morning! I had slept through what was to be our own fancy anniversary dinner. Norah had had a tomato sandwich. Needless to say, I have heard about that tomato sandwich on each of the subsequent anniversaries I have been fortunate enough to spend with Norah.

This brings us to 1974, which turned out to be a significant banner year for us with two positive banners and two negative ones. First the negative ones: early in the year Norah discovered a lump in her breast which turned out to be malignant and resulted in a massive single mastectomy precluding reconstruction. The second negative happened when we were visiting our good friends and former partners, Ann and Paul Anderson, in Rancho Santa Fe. I had been losing weight and not feeling well but it was nothing I could identify. Paul felt that I looked so bad he got up from dinner and called his doctor to make an appointment for me in the morning. After undergoing many tests at Scripps Hospital and Clinic the doctor determined that I had a rare blood disease, subacute bacterial endocarditis, which was serious for me because of my poor heart condition. It required seven weeks of hospitalization and huge doses of antibiotics intravenously. The hospital was seventy miles from our house on Balboa Island, but Norah drove it every day to visit me. The Andersons were great too, and it was a strange coincidence that I was given a room they had donated on the cardiac floor. It had a plaque with their name on the door.

The two positive banners of that year were first Cathy's graduation from Notre Dame (which we were able to attend) and our purchase of our own sailboat while I was in the hospital. I had heard that a neighbor on Balboa Island wanted to sell his thirty-six-foot Islander, so I asked Norah to go down and make a deal for it. We were fortunate to be able to get an excellent partner, Hobie Denny, to share the expense, so we acquired not only an excellent sailboat but an excellent friend as well. Hobie happened to be the commodore of one of the harbor's best yacht clubs, the Bahia Corinthian, so he facilitated our switching membership from Voyagers where I was having a little difficulty with the its commodore.

Cathy's graduation was the other positive highlight of the year. We were able to attend, and while there we had a party for Cathy's twenty-first birthday in our motel. The motel was twenty miles down the road from Notre Dame, so we didn't expect many of her friends to attend, but we were wrong; the party was jammed, showing how popular Cathy was with her classmates.

Cathy helped pay her way through Notre Dame with student loans she arranged herself and by teaching ice skating in the rink on campus. Shortly after she graduated there was a teaching job open at the Ice Capades Chalet in Charlotte, North Carolina, so I offered her the job. She was reluctant at first because most of her class mates were planning to play awhile down in Florida, but she agreed. A year or so later we opened another Chalet in La Jolla about seventy miles from our home so I offered her the chance to transfer there so she would be closer to home. But she turned me down with the statement, "I don't want to leave here, Dad. These southern gentlemen still open the car door for girls on a date!" And sure enough, a year later she met one, Jimmy Tanner, whom she married and made the father of three wonderful children.

Cathy was named after her mother, Catherine Norah Kirby, who is known as Norah; Cathy named her first daughter Catherine Norah Kirby Tanner, and she is known as Kirby. So there are three generations of family girls all with the same name, but each one uses a different part of it.

As with all other decisions in life, our move from the Chicago area to Balboa Island in California, had its up side and its down side. The down side was leaving so many great friends and moving farther away from Kenora, where we loved spending summer vacations with Tom and Tasie O'Flaherty, Norah's sister. In Chicago we were particularly close to Carol and Tom Barrett, whom we met as skating pupils in our Park Ridge skating school. We bought a small, eighteen-foot Lightning sailboat together and had many a fun time with it. When I called my sister Stephanie in Denver and mentioned that we were getting a sailboat she said, "I know the name of it. It must be called *Finally* since you have wanted a boat since you were a boy in Sydney." So with a slight nautical variation, we named the boat *Fine-A-Lee*.

With our mutual friends, the Nasharres and the Barretts, we made a one-day trip to Montreal to attend the international "Expo" of 1967. Paul Butler, owner of the Oakbrook Polo Club, gave Norah and I a guest membership, and the club arranged a charter flight leaving Chicago at dawn and returning at midnight. By coincidence it was Tony Nasharre's birthday, so we had quite a flying international birthday bash for Tony. We still miss our friends there, including the Barrets' close friend Father Jim Cross, whom we took sailing later on a visit to California, where we lost both the wind and the motor twenty miles out at sea and had to be towed back to harbor.

13

Decade Six 1975-1985

If there is a consistent theme to this decade, it is our period of sailing, racing, and cruising. A great many other important events took place at this time, but the sailing was the dominant activity. Hobie Denny was a good partner because of his many personal connections as an officer of the Bahia Corinthian Yacht Club. He brought in another partner, John Tatum, a young bachelor who loved to race and was very good at it. So we became frequent contenders for trophies in the races held by the various yacht clubs in Newport Harbor. There were overnight races around offshore islands such as Santa Catalina, twenty miles off Long Beach, and San Clemente Island about fifty miles off Newport, plus numerous races up and down the Coast or around buoys near the shore. The most exciting race was the annual Newport to Ensenada, sometimes called the Tequila Derby for obvious reasons. I crewed for Les Grant in three of them and then sailed in eleven more in our own thirty-six-foot Islander, which was now named *Stroker* thanks to John.

One of our most consistent and popular crew members who became our frequent cook (she called herself our galley slave!) was the young movie actress, Lynn Holly Johnson, who had started as a three-year-old toddler in our Park Ridge skating school. For some time she and our son David were skating pair partners, and in one early competition she even beat Tai Babalonia and Randy Gardner.

In addition to racing, *Stroker* was able to accommodate six to eight persons for overnight cruising. Our most frequent destination was Santa Catalina, where we could moor safely on one of their permanent moorings so we did not have to rely on the more indefinite anchoring. The only problem with Catalina, other than finding an available mooring on busy weekends, was the danger of Santa Ana winds. They are annual offshore winds that cause considerable damage and they blow directly into the many otherwise good anchorages on the south side of the island. Over the years we have been caught in three or four Santa Ana winds, and they have been scary. During one of them, even though we were on a secure mooring in Avalon Harbor, the harbor patrol woke us at three in the morning advising that we go around to the safer leeward side of the island. There were only three of us on board—M.J., Norah, and myself but with some difficulty we were able to free our mooring and head around the island. We had to take as wide a course as possible in case our engine failed—we would be blown back on the rocky shore. It took us six hours to go around to a small harbor, called Little Harbor, where we still put out two forward anchors because the wind was still so strong. Normally we could cover the distance in less than an hour. It was Thanksgiving weekend so we listened to the USC-Notre Dame game and enjoyed the comfort and snugness of our little safe haven. Another harrowing experience happened when Norah and I were bringing *Stroker* back from the Ensenada race. We had stopped overnight at the San Diego Yacht Club, which is most hospitable, and checked in with customs. Then we proceeded for a half day to Oceanside, which has a difficult harbor entrance but a pleasant harbor and comfortable restaurants. Before leaving the next morning we checked with the harbormaster about the weather up to Newport. They said everything looked fine, so we took off. About an hour or two out of Oceanside, the wind became very strong, right from the direction we were heading. It got so bad and strong, and the waves so big that we could only see one at a time coming straight for us. It was a rough ride, and at one point our headsail blew into pieces. I had to go forward to get it down so I tied myself to a lifeline and I tied Norah to the steering pedestal, the wheel, so the waves were crashing right back into the cockpit would not sweep her overboard. I was able to get the sail down and return to the cockpit safely, and relieve Norah. As we were approaching Dana Point Harbor, the next safe port, we came across a smaller catamaran (light, two-hulled) sailboat being powered by a small outboard motor and crewed by one man. As we approached we recognized Buddy Epsom, of *Beverly Hillbillies* fame and he asked us to stay with him in case he needed a tow into Dana Point. We did but he made it safely. We stayed overnight in a comfortable harbor dock slip next to each other, and the next morning he asked us to stay with him for the final fifteen miles to Newport in case the wind came up again. Buddy lived on Newport Bay and was an avid sailor and racer, but this storm was too much for his small racing boat.

There were many more sailing and racing stories to tell, but when it came time for us to move to San Diego we felt that we had finished our sailing days and would be satisfied with cruises on big boats.

Business Declining

During this period my business activities with *Ice Capades* began to run down. George decided that a man I had hired ten years earlier as a teacher and manager could assume the responsibility of operations manager for the Chalets, and that I could concentrate on new expansion. I did not feel the man was qualified to take on that responsibility, and I could not work with him. I made arrangements with George to resign as an employee and become a consultant for three years on new expansion. However, at the same time George decided to retire, and his vice president , Dick Palmer took over as president. I felt the personnel changes had taken away the momentum of what George and I had built in the Chalets, so I left as soon as my contract was up. I was right about momentum. When I left we had twenty successful Chalets but under the new management they not only did not grow, but they also began to diminish as many of them closed. When the company was sold a few years later, there were only twelve Chalets operating. This may sound like sour grapes, but it is a fact that the Chalets went down considerably after I left them. Two of them in Texas had been taken over by a company that hired my son David to run them. They are both doing triple the business they were doing under the last *Ice Capades* management.

Ernie Hahn

Before I retired, however, there were a couple of business developments that were particularly rewarding both economically and socially. One was meeting and doing business with one of the greatest men in the real estate construction and development business, Ernie Hahn, not only a great businessman but also a great philanthropist. He was a generous benefactor of the University of San Diego, among other charities. Ernie wanted to build a shopping center in La Jolla just north of San Diego, but the city and the University of California (which controlled the property), insisted that the development include 150,000 square feet of cultural and recreational amenities, including an ice rink so the school could develop a hockey team.

The Hahn company contacted me to do a feasibility study for the ice rink. I remember the first time they took me to the proposed site, and standing on the highest spot I could not see a building of any kind in any direction. I asked how could they know this was a good shopping center site and they simply said, "Because Mr. Hahn says it is!" I did my study of the demographics and traffic exposure, et cetera, and came up with an estimated annual revenue for the ice rink of only about $300,000—which would be marginal and not support the value of the space it would need. However, Hahn decided to proceed, partly due to pressure from the community, so we entered into our first lease with him. Two years later when the center was completed the Ice Capades Chalet did an annual sales volume in excess of twice what I had predicted. As a result we ended up leasing six more Chalets at Hahn Centers. In fact, in one afternoon, George Eby and I negotiated preliminary terms for a total of seventeen centers. It was quite a business deal involving millions of dollars, and it was only possible because Ernie and George were such astute and yet reasonable businessmen. We have lost both of these fine gentlemen in recent years, and their professions, their families, and their many friends, will miss them for years to come, as I do personally very deeply.

The seventeen centers never developed because Ernie sold his company to Trizec Development of Canada, and they must have had enough ice skating in Canada and did not want any in their centers. Ernie felt that the ice skating was a great addition to the entire center and thus could justify the fact that it did not pay for the large space it took up in the center. At one of the annual conventions of the International Council of Shopping Centers, Ernie was on one of the large, important panels, and the others were questioning his desire for ice skating since they knew that the rink wasn't justifying its space in the center. Ernie began his remarks by saying he hoped Michael Kirby wasn't in the audience since we were talking about negotiating some new leases. He went on to say that when a food court, which is the conglomeration of fast food sales booths usually in the center of a mall, was overlooking the ice skating, the sales of food per square foot doubled over the average mall without skating. So the rent he didn't get from the ice area was more than made up by the additional percentage rent he had from the food court. He also felt that if there were two or more malls in a town, people would identify more with the one with the ice skating since it made it distinctive. We ended up building seven ice chalets in Hahn malls, and they all did better than most of the others.

South Africa

The other example of fine business and interesting deal was our sale of a franchise for an ice skating facility in Johannesburg, South Africa, for the Anglo-American Mining Company, which markets DeBeers diamonds. They had an office, hotel, and underground shopping center in downtown Johannesburg which was completely built up, so the only place for the ice rink was the top floor of a parking structure adjoining the complex. We helped design and construct the rink and set up its operation, so I had to make a number of trips to South Africa, and they were all most pleasant because of the people with whom I had to work. Nigel Mandy was the general manager of the entire complex, and he had become interested in adding ice skating after he visited our Chalet at the Houston Galleria. His wife Lida, son Stephen, and daughter Lorna, all became good friends with our family. They all visited with us at our home in Balboa Island, and one summer our son Christopher spent with the Mandys and worked at the rink. He would drive in with Mandy in his Mercedes then get into work clothes and drive the Zamboni to resurface the ice.

Ice Capades had agreed to the franchise with the assurance that no person would be excluded from using the facility. However, the apartheid laws required certain restrictions. With the strong help of Mandy, we were able to affect some compromises. We had to supply "coloreds" with a separate set of rental skates (which we didn't), and separate wash rooms, which we designated in hockey dressing rooms but didn't bother policing, so there was no difficulty. It became a very successful operation.

Our parent company, Metromedia, told us to give up the franchise three years later because there was so much antipathy to

South Africa in America that they were afraid of repercussions against their television stations.

The Mandys had a dinner party for Chief Mangosuthu Buthelezi of the Zulu tribe, the largest in South Africa, which was attended by the chief and about twenty of his entourage, all decked out in their native tribal robes. I had the pleasure of sitting across the table from the chief during dinner and had a very interesting and enlightening conversation with him.

The chief was educated at Oxford in England, so he is very erudite. He asked me about the civil rights movement in the United States, since our meeting was only a few years after the tumultuous sixties. He claimed that the so-called "civil rights movement" had misconstrued the American concept of apartheid, which had only been an official law in South Africa since 1948. The comparison of our civil rights problems with theirs in South Africa was wrong because his people were so illiterate and uneducated that they had no concept of a country called South Africa; they only knew that they lived in the Zulu homeland, Kwazulu, and they would only do what their chief, himself, told them to do. For this reason he said a much more apt comparison would be for us to compare their social situation today to the situation in America in the sixteenth and seventeenth centuries, when we were dealing with the Indians, the so-called Native Americans. They were divided into different tribes, always fighting just as the African tribes were divided and fighting today. He correctly pointed out that we had no intention in those days to incorporate the Indians into our voting population or any other facet of government. In fact, the opposite was true when we tried to separate them onto reservations, which is similar to the South African government's attempt to set up "homelands" for the various tribes in their country.

Chief Buthelezi went so far as to say that apartheid was good for his people and, in fact, it was mutual. Since the Zulu wars with the English and Dutch in the nineteenth century, which the Zulus almost won, they still looked with contempt on the white man and felt superior to him. Certainly, this was a different and unpromoted consideration than that by the English- and Dutch-controlled establishment. It is coincidental perhaps that the same type of thinking is being promulgated in the concept of Afrocentrism promoted by much of academia, which claim that

Aristotle and Cleopatra, among other famous figures in history, were actually black.

A couple of incidents occurred, one amusing, that were particular to South Africa. Mandy wanted to consider adding an ice skating facility to some property his company owned in the city of Durban. He asked me to go over there with him to evaluate the property. While we were having lunch in a very attractive resort overlooking the ocean, I confessed that I wasn't sure if Durban was far enough south to be on the Indian or Atlantic Ocean. He suggested that I ask the waiter. When I asked the waiter, "Is this the Indian Ocean?" the waiter said, "Oh no, sir, this is the white beach. The Indian is about a mile up the road." Indians formed a large part of the population since the British had imported them from India for labor needed to develop the gold and diamond mines they had discovered. Large numbers of them had intermarried with the local black population to form a distinct ethnic group known as "coloreds." So they were discriminated against, although not as severely as the blacks.

The other incident occurred when the Mandys invited me to spend a weekend with them visiting the Krueger National Park, a refuge for the wildlife of Africa in the northeast part of the country bordering on Mozambique. Unfortunately, Mozambique had recently installed a Communist government, which stopped their mosquito abatement program, resulting in a huge increase in the mosquito population. Since the mosquitoes did not know about the border, the increase spread over into the Krueger Park, and since the mosquito is the carrier of malaria, any visitor to the park had to take a malaria protection medical program—which required three weeks of shots and medication both before and after the visit. Despite the inconvenience and discomfort of the medical program, the visit to the park was well worthwhile. A beautiful leopard practically ran under our car; the baboons were bold, and the giraffes in mating season gave meaning to the word "necking." The cottages we stayed in looked like native thatched huts but actually include all the finest accommodations. The visit and the drive to and from the park were fitting endings to the excitement and pleasure of a country with a most interesting and misunderstood culture and history.

Returning from one of my visits to South Africa, Norah and I made arrangements to meet in Europe. She was going over with her good friend Wina Richardson, so we arranged to meet in

Lausanne. My flight landed in Zurich, and I was to take a train to meet them. When I got to the train station in Zurich I saw trains to Lugano, Lucerne, and Lausanne, and I suddenly wasn't sure which one we had agreed upon. Fortunately, I guessed correctly and they were waiting for me at the Lausanne station. We made our first visit to Champery, where Denise Eby's sister had a beautiful Chalet.

While South Africa was one of the more interesting locations for our developing Ice Capades Chalets, we were still involved in developing others, particularly with the Ernie Hahn company. We opened chalets in Dallas, Prestonwood Shopping Center, Memphis, Portland, Oregon, Clackamas Town Center (where the infamous Tonya Harding discovered ice skating), San Mateo on the San Francisco peninsula, Palos Verdes adjacent to Los Angeles and the last one I did for *Ice Capades*, Palm Desert Town Center here in the Coachela Valley near Palm Springs and our home in La Quinta.

During this time George gave up the presidency to Dick Palmer, who was also a friend of ours. George retained an interest in the Chalets, however, so we still worked together, although it was winding down for both of us. Dick never seemed enthused about the Chalet program and was not aggressive for growth, which was all I had been doing for them. In fact, he began a policy of retrenchment and voluntarily closed some units down. I had resigned as an employee but was retained for three years at my request under a consulting contract. This gave both George and me more time for ourselves and we went on a number of cruises together.

George and I joked about the new Chalet in the desert, where we both wanted to retire. We argued over which of us would be able to manage the Palm Desert Chalet to help our retirement income. A couple of amusing incidents occurred shortly after the Chalet opened.

I had disagreed with Ernie about having an ice skating facility in the desert; I claimed that there were only old retired people there who didn't skate and wanted to get away from ice and snow. I conducted a feasibility study, which confirmed that there wasn't enough population to fit our profile of what was necessary. But Ernie insisted and proved to be right. It was much more successful than I had predicted.

We held a charity ice show, which was a big local event for the Betty Ford Clinic nearby. Ernie had a reception afterwards for all the main supporters, and during it he came over to me and said, "Michael, please tell me where else I shouldn't build an ice rink!" Also that night I was announcing from rinkside, and Betty and former President Ford were sitting right beside me. As they went by I welcomed them and mentioned my name. Well, President Ford put his arm around me and exclaimed how good it was to see me again! Of course he had never seen me before in his life, but the old politician was coming out.

One of my greatest pleasures with retirement was being able to spend more time with the boat and my friends at Bahia Corinthian Yacht Club. A couple of men who worked a four-day week started meeting regularly at the club on Fridays for lunch. We began to call ourselves "The Friday Lunch Bunch" and became quite notorious. We frequently went to a local restaurant, a different one each week. Someone had the opportunity to buy an old Cadillac limousine, so we chipped in and bought it to get to our weekly luncheon. It was a fun group, and some remnants of it still meet occasionally at the club. But unfortunately it has been diminished by death and moves away such as ours. About the time I retired in 1980, Denise had the idea of taking a cruise in the eastern Mediterranean and invited us to join them. So we booked a two-week cruise out of Athens on the *Stella Solaris* and toured the Aegean visiting Mykanos, Santorini, Rhodes, Ephesus and Istanbul. It was our first cruise, and we fell in love with it. After the cruise we flew to Geneva on our way to a chalet, a real Swiss one. On arrival at the Geneva airport while we were waiting for our luggage, Norah looked up at the conveyor belt, and nudged George and said, "Oh, look George. Denise's suitcase is snuggling up to yours—isn't that cute?"

George looked up and without batting an eye said, "Yeah, but not in a very sexy position." You can see why we had fun traveling with them.

After the cruise Denise and George took us to the chalet of her sister Francine, in the little village of Champery about three thousand feet up the mountain near Geneva. We loved that too and tried to go there every time we were in Europe. We had most of our family meet us there a few years later, and Cathy named the hill we had to walk up to the chalet Killer Hill. It was still called that a couple of years ago when Denise arranged for Norah and I to celebrate our fiftieth wedding anniversary there. Champery is the start of the *telepherique*, the aerial tramway that carries skiers and tourists up to the twelve-thousand-foot peak of the mountain. Since Tommy was the youngest, the others would send him up to the top early in the morning to report on weather conditions up there. After a week or so of skiing and walking and just enjoying the mountain scenery, we then had a delightful drive around Italy and France staying in real chateaux and eating regional menu meals. However, the first thing Tommy did when we arrived in Paris was to find a local Big Mac!

A couple of years after our first cruise, Denise suggested another cruise. She was becoming our unofficial tour director. This time it was from Hamburg up the coast of Norway to the North Cape, the northern most point in Europe. It, too, was a most beautiful trip, but I had an unfortunate incident before leaving that put a damper on the trip for me. I had just had my annual physical exam with a new set of doctors since I was no longer an employee of *Ice Capades*. The cardiologist reported that I had to have a heart operation as soon as possible. He made it sound very serious. When I told him we were leaving in a day or so for this cruise, and would be gone almost a month, he prescribed some medication that I was to take four times daily. As the cruise wore on I began feeling worse and worse and was sure the doctor had been right and I should have had the operation. But I lasted through the cruise and afterwards a drive across Germany and France to the real chalet in Champery. On the day we returned home I began to bleed for no apparent reason and went to a doctor who discovered that I was allergic to the medication the heart doctor had given me just before leaving on the trip. My regular cardiologist also confirmed that I did not really need a heart operation yet. The other doctor nearly did me in; I wish now that I had thought of malpractice then.

14

Personal Matters

The most serious event of this decade was the death of our son Terry. Terry had been living in Chicago with Tricia and Denny for awhile, but later on his own. We were able to visit him at least once a year on our travels, and we saw enough of him to know that he had a serious drinking and maybe drug problem. One day Norah took a phone call and came out screaming to me to take it. It was a hospital in Chicago saying Terry had been admitted the previous night after a very serious accident that may be life-threatening. We immediately arranged to fly to Chicago and got there early the next morning. Terry was in intensive care but seemed to be in good spirits. He said he did not know how he got there. They had not fully assessed his damages, but it turned out that he had had a bad fall or jumped from a third-floor balcony onto a concrete deck after fighting with his girlfriend. He had a broken back and numerous internal injuries. His company on the Chicago Stock Exchange had very good insurance on him, so they were taking care of all expense. Terry spent about six months having operations and recuperating. We eventually brought him out to Balboa Island and rented a house behind ours for him and Tom, who was still in college nearby. He told Tricia he wanted to die, and one time he took a complete bottle of valium pills with a full bottle of vodka, which we did not know how he got because we hid any liquor we had. One night Tom came home and found him wandering in the alley not knowing which house was his or ours. Tom took him to the hospital, where they diagnosed a brain aneurysm that had developed from the accident and was probably too small for the doctors in Chicago to detect. Tom woke us up and took us to the hospital at three in the morning. The neurologist advised that they could operate but there was a good chance that Terry could end up being a vegetable. I said that we should give God a little more time. The doctor called at ten the next morning saying that Terry had passed away. I will never know if I made the right decision, and it still haunts me. Terry was always too self-effacing to the point of having an inferiority complex. Although he was a well-known junior hockey star in Chicago, he would not go to the Chicago Black Hawks professional hockey team training camp when I arranged it for him because he said he was not ready. Terry was extremely well-liked and successful on LaSalle Street, the Wall Street of Chicago, especially the Chicago Board of Options Exchange, and he spoke of someday buying his own seat. But when I offered to help him do so he would say the same thing: "I'm not ready yet—maybe next year." On 6 December 1984, the good Lord decided there would be no "next year" for Terry on this earth, so I hope he is enjoying the ultimate eternal stock market up there.

Early in 1987 I was walking home from the club and suddenly felt very weak; the bridge to Balboa Island had a slight rise to it, and I felt I was climbing a mountain. I had to rest on the sea wall every few feet the rest of the way home. I just decided to rest and went to bed for the rest of the day. The next morning, however, my pulse was speeding and I felt shortness of breath, so I had Norah call the doctor, and of course they told me to come in. As Norah drove the seventy miles to the hospital in La Jolla, I was more worried about dying in a car accident than from my heart. She must have been going a hundred most of the way. It turned out to be heart failure rather than a heart attack so I had to be admitted. A couple of days later things seemed to be normal so my doctor said that since I would have to have a heart operation sooner or later I might as well have it now. So I said go for it. On 7 February I was given a mechanical aorta heart valve. I was discharged on 14 February. It has worked fine ever since, so far.

Fortunately, later that year, our tour leader, Denise, came up with another grand cruise. We flew Singapore Airlines to Tokyo, spent three days there, then took the bullet train to the ancient capital of Kyoto for a couple more days. Next we boarded the *Royal Princess* for fifteen days to San Francisco, with only one stop for a few hours in Honolulu. Our friend Susan Davis was visiting there, so we had a pleasant visit and lunch with her.

It was on this cruise that George pulled one of his humorous stunts on me. At the time he first hired me to develop the Chalet

Skating School Program, I tried to claim that since my teaching system was copyrighted, I should get a royalty from its use in addition to my salary. George was smart enough not to agree to that, so it never occurred. But one night during dinner on the cruise when we were talking about old times, I asked him if he would have agreed to the royalty if I had insisted. He just smiled enigmatically. After dinner when we were having a brandy, he said, "If I answered your question it would probably ruin the rest of the cruise for you." Well, of course that answer didn't ruin the cruise, but it sure made me think!

San Diego Ice Arena

Still later in the year 1987, another event came up which was to have serious and costly consequences for us.

Our son, David and his lovely wife Holly were teaching in Troy, Ohio, and were active with the committee putting on the 1987 World Figure Skating Competition in Cincinnati. A skating friend of theirs who was teaching in San Diego and visiting the Worlds introduced David to the owner of the arena there because she felt that it needed a male teacher and hoped he would consider it. David asked me to meet with the owner and look over the situation in San Diego. So in March, a month after my heart operation while I was still recuperating, I drove down to meet the owner, Hank Gotthelf. He owned the arena because he had bought acreage from a bank to build houses. The bank had foreclosed on it, and the arena was included. Hank was not an operator or manager. It turned out that neither David nor I could work there because of an agreement we had with *Ice Capades* not to operate or manage any ice facility within ten miles of an *Ice Capades* operation, and the arena happened to be just within ten miles of the Ice Capades Chalet I had built for Ernie at the University Town Center in La Jolla. So that ended that.

But six months later Hank called me to ask if I would come down and help him with the management of the ice arena. We worked out a deal under which I would be a consultant spending some time each month analyzing the rink operation and making suggestions on how it might be improved. The operation was a mess with no adequate managing or control. In fact, the evening manager was selling beer to hockey players on the premises for her own account in violation of her position and many local laws.

Hank was in serious jeopardy and was losing money at the rate of twenty-five thousand dollars per month. I worked with his accountant on the books, so I knew this was accurate. After two or three months it became obvious that Hank was not implementing the changes I recommended, so I told him he was wasting his money paying me a fee and not doing anything about it.

Included in my reports to him was a three-year projection, which showed that the arena business could be tripled and made profitable in two years. Hank and his partner asked if I would take it over and do that. I said I would if they made me a reasonable offer. They offered me a twelve-year lease but divided it into three-year segments, which they said was required by their banker. It was the worst business deal I ever made. I felt Hank was honest and truthful and that I was saving him thousands of dollars each month plus a lot of his time and possible criminal exposure for the activities of his personnel. I discovered at great personal expense that he was not honest, truthful, or appreciative.

We invested considerably in items that would improve the operation, such as about $50,000 on energy saving methods (which actually paid for themselves in two years), plus many other improvements, including an extensive advertising and promotion program.

My main incentive in taking on this business was the lease-option to buy the property, especially if it improved as much as I predicted. It did, and we became profitable in eighteen months. Hank maintained a close personal relationship with the teacher who had introduced us and who was still on the staff. I imagine she kept giving Hank reports on how the business was improving. He could see it as we had to pay percentage rent on increased volume, and she could take it over now. On the second anniversary Hank gave us notice that since I did not pick up the option to purchase the property, he would exercise his right to cancel the lease in one year; which he did. He disputed our profit figures on which he was to pay for the cancellation right. He also disputed the claims we had to be reimbursed for all the improvements we put in. Since January is the first month of the year that enables us to begin collecting enough cash flow to pay bills that have been accumulating since the low summer business, Hank's termination in January and disputed payments to us required us to file for Chapter Eleven bankruptcy. We were operating as a sole proprietorship which meant that the bankruptcy affected our personal credit reports.

We finally found a lawyer who would take the case on consignment, and almost five years later we collected fifty thousand dollars from Hank. The lawyer got twenty thousand, so we ended up with about twenty percent of our investment, which the current operators, the girlfriend's friends, are still benefiting from. We not only stopped his monthly losses, which would have been close to one million dollars if we had not taken over the business, plus he is now getting the benefit of the improvements we made. Nice guy.

But the nicest thing that happened to us from the move to San Diego was joining the parish of St. Gregory the Great, which we happened to move into when we bought our condo in Promontory Point in the Scripps Ranch district. We had made a very good sale of our property on Balboa Island and would have been well off except for having put so much of it into the ice arena. The beauty of St. Gregory was its young pastor, Father Jim Poulsen. We still consider him one of our best friends and use every excuse to visit Tom and Cyndi in San Diego so we can visit with him and the many friends we still know at the parish. They all make us feel like it's old home week every time we stop there.

Another pleasant thing that happened during our stay in San Diego was being re-united with another dear friend, Dede Dahlberg, now Disbrow. Dede was a close friend of Libby McFadden, who was teaching at one of our skating schools in the Chicago area in the early 1960s, and she wanted to start a teaching career of her own, preferably with her friend Libby. I gave her first teaching job and helped her learn about it. Well, years later she was attending a professional skaters convention in San Diego and invited us down to the hotel for a drink. When she saw that I was wearing hearing aids, she asked if I needed new ones, and by coincidence I did so. She offered to get them for me since her family owned the Miracle Ear company, which made an excellent hearing aid. Dede arranged for me to be fitted at the local distributor, and when I went to pay for them there was no charge. In talking to Dede she said that I had done her a favor in starting her teaching career and this was a way she could thank me!

Return to Sonja's Norway

In 1992 Norwegian television asked to interview me for a special they were doing on Sonja. I was also asked to be a guest at her museum to help celebrate her eightieth anniversary. So I went to Norway in June 1992 for the event with strict instructions from Norah and her friends to find accommodations for them for the Winter Olympics to be held in Norway in February 1994. Through the help of the director of the museum, a meeting was set for me with two executives of the Olympic Organizing Committee in the town of Hamar, which was to host the figure skating and speed skating competitions. Hamar is about an hour by train from Oslo and near the town of Lillehammer, which was the official Olympic venue for most of the other winter sports. I went with Reidar Borjeson, another skater I had met at the Worlds in Norway in 1954 forty years earlier.

We were met at the station in Hamar by Ola Rinnan, the banker who arranged most of the financing for the venues being built in Hamar for the skating events. He took us to his office, where we were joined by Hans Erick, the contractor in charge of construction. We had a pleasant lunch in Ola's office, where we discussed possible places to stay for the Olympics. Towards the end of the meal Ola asked us if we would be interested in staying in a couple of farms. I had told them that we expected our group to be about twenty persons. The thought of "farms" brought images of cows, pigs, and manure to mind, but since they seemed sincere about it I decided to be polite and say yes we would. After lunch Ola made a quick phone call in Norwegian and then took us in his BMW to see the ice rinks under construction. They were most impressive; especially the larger one called the Viking Skipet, because it resembled a Viking ship upside down on the beach. It covered a total of five acres under roof with not one single pillar and included a full skating racing oval plus other ice rinks and a soccer field in the center. It is a most impressive building. The other rink under construction was a more conventional arena with about six thousand seats and built for hockey and figure skating events.

As we drove into the second site we were met at the entrance by an attractive woman who gave Ola a large envelope. When we had seen the building Ola asked if we would like to see the farms, so we of course said yes.

It turned out that both farms were about a five-minute drive out of Hamar, and they certainly put my concept of a farm to shame. The Rinnans owned one of them, called Smedstua, and it consisted of five buildings, including a separate Norwegian dining hall called a Stabbur. It was an estate, not a farm, and it could easily accommodate ten guests. The other one was owned by Hans Erick, and it was nearly as nice and also could accommodate ten guests. I found out what the rent would be and converting it to U.S. dollars figured out it would be a bargain for everyone. So I made a tentative agreement with Ola that day to book the farms for the Olympics. I found out later that the woman who met us at the construction site was Ola's wife, Anna Lin, and he had apparently decided during lunch that we could be satisfactory tenants for their property, and that is why he decided to show me the farms. A great many details had to be worked out, and Ola and I exchanged many letters, faxes, and phone calls during the next two years. I said the entire deal was dependent on our ability to get tickets to the figure skating events and Ola and Hans guaranteed they would get them for us. They did because every Norwegian was given priority for a certain number of tickets so Ola and Hans prevailed on their friends and employees to order tickets for us if they were not going to use them. We ended up with well over two hundred tickets, which was more than we needed.

We realized that we had to put a complete package together including transportation, tickets, and accommodations, and that we needed a travel agency for that. We also needed to finance the advance needs of the project. The deposits for the farms had to be met early before we could receive any deposits from customers, and the tickets also had to be paid for well in advance before the package could be sold.

I contacted a couple of travel agencies I knew, including one in the east which was owned by a USFSA official. When I offered the package to him, he told me I had to be lying because they could not get the number of tickets I claimed that I had. I was able to get Bryan Travel in San Francisco interested although they were skeptical because they had been burned on the tickets promised them for the 1988 Olympics in Calgary. But Joan Burns and Harry (of Bryan) went to Norway and checked out the farms as well as the ticket availability, and they were convinced that what I had said was true. So they put a very generous package together and sold it to many of their customers, as well as our friends who had asked me to put the package together. The package soon sold out to many people we did not know, but fortunately they all turned out to be wonderful people.

Norah and I flew to Norway a week before the Olympics were to start to be sure all the farms were complete, et cetera. The producer of the television special on Sonja, Edvard Hambo, invited us to his house for a salmon dinner he prepared because he knew I loved the Norwegian Salmon. He also knew of my interest in a biography of Sonja, so he asked me how it was coming and whether I would consider using Tonya Harding as Sonja in any movie that might develop. The Tonya Harding-Nancy Kerrigan incident had just happened a couple of weeks earlier. I said, "Sure, Tonya is bad enough to be a good Sonja." Edvard's girlfriend was there and asked me if I would say that on the air. She had a morning radio talk show. So I agreed and she got her recording equipment from the car. We recorded an interview right in the living room. She played the interview on her show the next morning. That day Norah and I were driving up to Hamar and when we got there about noon there were five requests for interviews with me from newspapers and television stations. I did most of them in the next couple of days and had a great deal of exposure on the Sonja project.

Many of those who made this tour are still communicating in one way or another. Anna Lin Rinnan had a good friend who is a world famous doctor of clinical psychology, Froydis Hogetveit, who is also an excellent cook and offered to cook for us while we were at Smedstua. Her meals were beyond perfection, and we ate like kings. We also enjoyed the friendship she shared with us. We all have maintained more than just contact with Froydis and the others but have developed enduring friendships. Ann Frick, one of our friends from the Los Angeles area, has visited Norway twice (including last Christmas) to visit with Froydis and her family, and Froydis has visited us in the Southern California area three times. It seems that almost all of the people who were on that trip have developed friendships with others on it, and we enjoy the memory of them all. Others from the group number her among our best friends. A coincidence about the Dalton location skating school near Chicago happened many years later when Norah and I took this group of people to the Winter Olympics in 1994 in Norway. One of the group, Naomi Zimbler, had grown interested in skating as a pupil of ours in Dalton. We became close friends of Naomi's and still keep in touch, even though she now lives in Minneapolis.

It is fitting that this narrative should end on a Norwegian note, as it started. These friendships are really all the responsibility of Sonja Henie, for whom this story was created. But it is not a story, it is a revelation of love and respect, now personified by all the Norwegian alliances that are living and developing all because of the influence of the remarkable Sonja Henie. I hope I have done her memory justice.

In addition to the effect of Sonja Henie on the lives of the people in the narrative, I hope that the reader has learned and understood the tremendous effect people have had on the lives of the protagonists of this revelation. In review I do not think the author has fairly described the wonderful influence on our lives by many of the people casually mentioned above. Therefore I would like to add an epilogue in which I can more properly describe their effect on these lives.

❧ *Epilogue* ❦

If you have read the above and not realized that we believe that the people we have known, including family and friends, are the ones who are responsible for anything of importance we have accomplished in life, then I have failed to express our true feelings about them and the obligation we feel towards them. As I review the instances recorded above with these persons, I am aware that I have not done justice to our obligation and gratitude for the importance of the actions they have taken that accrued so much to our benefit.

A professor at the College of the Desert which I have been attending gave a very moving anecdote which expresses our feelings on the people we have tried to portray as the real reasons for any success we have achieved in life. During his introductory lecture he told the story of how poor his family was so that his chance of going to college was very slim. But a family friend knew of his desire to study music in hopes that it could bring some good to mankind, so he told young John that he would pay his way through college and that John had no obligation to pay him back except to do a great job with his music. Professor John told us that that opportunity opened up his world for him. He said that he paid back every penny that the man had advanced for his education but he also went on to say, "But I never really paid that man back for what he really gave me." That is the way I feel about the many people I have written about in this story. As I review it I realize that in so many of the references to the people in our lives I have not come close to fully expressing the importance of what they have given us, or more importantly the gratitude we feel for what they have done for us. Consequently, I would like to ask your indulgence in this epilogue as I try to review and emphasize their importance to us.

First, let me establish that the frequent replacement with the singular and plural personal pronouns throughout the text is intentional, because the "we" is not the imperial singular but rather the reference to us as a married team. Norah and I have been so close for so many years and shared our work as well as private lives that the "we" and "I" become interchangeable and indistinguishable. As I stated briefly and not emphatically enough, this singular life did not begin until it became a part of the life of Norah McCarthy. In fact, our concept of marriage is that it is not just a fifty-fifty affair, but rather a 100-100 condition in which we each must contribute one hundred percent of ourselves to the construction and success of the marriage, which becomes almost a separate third entity in our lives.

The next most important group of persons to influence our lives are five father figures, including primarily my real father, Fred L. Kirby. The middle initial is for Luke, and my father claimed that at the seventh or eighth child his parents were running out of saints' names. The most notable characteristic of my father's life with his family was how badly he was maligned by it, myself included. It was not until many years later when I experienced the vicissitudes of marriage and parenthood that I realized how wrong I had been in my feeling towards my father. Now I think of him as the loving , kind, and patient genius he must have been. I am frequently reminded of things he told me that seemed so obvious and simple at the time but are still needed today. Automobile horns annoy me beyond reason, because when he was teaching me to drive, at about twelve years of age, he always said that the horn could never replace the brake. He also said that one must never run across a street. I did not understand this for years until I figured out that if you could not walk slowly across, then traffic was too heavy to do so. In addition to the immense support and sacrifice he made for my skating, he taught me a love for good music by osmosis as he listened to symphony orchestras every Sunday on the radio. Sometimes on those Sundays he would teach me to play chess, which I still like today. And although I am not good at math I'll never forget the six-by-seven multiplication table from one Sunday he drilled it into me. He introduced me to a few writers whom I didn't appreciate or understand at the time but whom I still enjoy today, Robert Benchley; P.G. Wodehouse and his fictional butler Jeeves; and Charles Lamb's essays, especially "The Origin of Roast Pork." It took me years to realize and appreciate so many things about him. My father died when I was only twenty-five, and I had been away with the ice shows for almost ten years, so I guess I just never really knew my father. It was not until many years later when I realized how many of his ideas I had incorporated into my life that I began to appreciate what a great person he was.

When I realize how my father must have suffered at the actions of my mother in her devotion to her own family instead of him and her defense of her actions at his expense to her children, I regret being so nonunderstanding at the time. He was a great man, far greater than he was ever given credit for. I also attribute to him, although in a somewhat subliminal way, my desire early in life to be a husband and father which I consider to be my most important if not most successful accomplishment in this life. So many times during my career have I wished he was around for help and advice. One of my greatest regrets was being unable to attend his funeral, when he died of throat cancer at the young age of fifty-four, in 1950. I was in my first year in London doing fifteen performances in every six-day week of *Rose Marie on Ice* and making more money than I had ever made for my own family. At least I had been able to visit him in the hospital in Toronto before I left for England.

Having just criticized my mother for her inordinate devotion and reliance on her family, I now have to admit that the next three father figures who helped and influenced my life were her father, John R. McIsaac, and her two brothers, Ronald and John. The three of them, as with one voice, taught me the meaning and value of our religious faith in building a strong family atmosphere. John R, although a busy executive with a strenuous and serious job, still found time for daily Mass, and on Sundays after Mass we would all go out to the cemetery and visit the family plot with the graves of two children who had died as babies. I used to wonder why we were standing around the graves praying when it was obvious that it was too late; they were dead! But it did give me a respect for death, and later I understood the importance of those prayers.

Ronald was the *bon vivant* of the family with his red convertible, and its rumbleseat, and his beautiful girlfriend, Norma Buckley. I can still see his trousers trembling during the wedding service when they were married. I've told you how he saved our house with his postdated checks, but there were many other instances of help from him.

John, who became Father John, and still is, was never Uncle John or just John, as the others wanted to be called; he was and still is in retirement the serious one. But as a scholar he gave me an interest in literature, especially G. K. Chesterton, whom I still enjoy.

One thing about friends is that when they are tried, true, and close, they are really family members. My next two father figures, Paul Anderson and George Eby, fit into that category. As I mentioned, the biggest business mistake I made was not entering into a closer business relationship with Paul. We became very close personally, and he was godfather to our son David Paul, or Paul David, as he called him. We were so pleased with our move to California since it enabled us to regain our friendship with Paul and Ann, who had moved here shortly before we did.

George Eby, who as president of *Ice Capades* was my immediate boss for twenty years, also became friendly enough to be considered family. When we both retired from *Ice Capades* we spent many vacations together and cruised both Atlantic and Pacific. We both moved to the desert at about the same time, and we still consider Denise Eby a best friend and are pleased that we only live five minutes apart so we can see each other frequently.

Almost in the category of a surrogate father was Arthur Wirtz, Sonja's producer. I worked for him for seven years without anything written on paper. It was all done with a handshake including the movie so it is obvious what an honorable person he was.

The next group of friends, and other "fathers," would have to be the many priests we have known who have played an important part in shaping our lives. My uncle, Father John, gave us one of the most awe-inspiring days in our lives. A woman in a small town north of Toronto but still in its diocese developed the Stigmata, the duplication of the wounds of Christ from the Crucifixion. The Catholic Church does not officially recognize the Stigmata, but the Cardinal Archbishop of Toronto asked Father John to be his liaison with the woman because her name, Mclsaac, was the same as his, although they were not related. One Friday when the woman suffered the pain of the Passion, Father John invited us to attend. We drove about an hour out of Toronto to a small farm cottage, where the woman lived with her husband and a number of children. At noon the woman retired to her small bedroom, and we were offered a place on our knees at the foot of her bed. Father John, another priest, and a few (maybe six or seven) other people crowded into the room. The woman started to cry and writhe around the bed, and we could see blood coming from her hands and her forehead. One of her daughters sat near the head of the bed and kept the bed covers so that they covered her mother at all times. The girl was reading a comic book. The mother's agony kept up for three hours, sometimes reaching a screaming level; when this happened one of the priests would stand by the bed and bless her with the sign of the cross. Although the woman had her eyes closed the entire time and frequently faced away from the priest, she would bless herself with the sign of the cross at the same time and would seem to calm down. The entire afternoon was a harrowing and hallowing time for us. The woman claimed that she had seen a vision of the Blessed Virgin, who spoke to her and told her to write down what she said. The woman did not have any paper except the missal she was reading, and she had nothing to write with but she took a comb from her hair and wrote the words by pressing it down on the soft blank pages at the front of the missal. When Father John took the missal to the cardinal, he had the impressions translated by experts, and it turned out that they were in Aramaic, which was the language spoken at the time of Christ. The woman was hardly literate in English, so she could not have made it up. The whole scene was a phenomenon that defies description. We never heard about the woman and what happened to her.

The other priests in our lives were more conventional. At St. Michael's I was only taught by priests, and they were all great guys, especially Father Norbert Clemens, who started me on histrionic phases of my career. He got me involved in acting in school plays and debating in the debating club. Both of these contributed to my later ability to act in movies and on stage as well as my time as a television announcer.

The priest who married us was a navy chaplain, Father Tom Reardon, who was on sick leave for malaria which he had contracted during the battle for Guadalcanal. He was not sure how long his leave would be, so that is why we were married on the inconvenient day of 23 December just before Christmas.

The summer of 1950 when I was in London by myself, I met an American priest who was studying family life in Ireland. At one meeting he asked me who was bringing up my family, and I, of course, answered Norah. He went on to ask me what I was doing about the family, and I said I was sending home the largest paycheck I ever had. He said something I'll never forget: "If you think that fulfills your obligation as a father, you are making a horrible mistake!" That festered within me for a year or more, especially since the show was making more demands on my time. I was anxious to spend more time with the family and I was anxious to start my new idea.

Another priest who helped me in the acting department, was Father Karl Schroeder of Loras College in Dubuque, Iowa. Father Karl was associated in some official capacity with the National Catholic Theater Association. They were holding an annual conference in Los Angeles one year, and I decided to attend to find out just what they did; I did not see much Catholic influence in the theater that I was exposed to. At the conference I had occasion to voice some of these concerns, and that attracted the attention of Father Karl. We got along very well and became good friends. He visited me in London when I was doing *Rose Marie*, and I visited him in Dubuque, which was only a couple of hours drive from Chicago. The crèche we still display at Christmas is one of the hand-carved figures which he brought back from Germany on one of his trips. I'd guess it is more than forty years old.

A priest who was probably closer to us as family was Father John Fahey. We first met through the Pre-Cana organization in Chicago. Pre-Cana consisted of four meetings in a week for engaged couples. They met at the church on a Sunday afternoon for a talk from a priest. Then, on Monday evening a married couple talked to them about the practical side of being married. On Wednesday a doctor talked about medical requirements of marriage, and on Friday the priest wrapped it all up for the couples. Father Fahey was one of the priests and we were one of the couples, so we got to know him well. He also taught a marriage course at Loyola University in Chicago and would have us give a guest lecture to those classes. The amazing coincidence, however, was that when he decided to retire from teaching he was assigned as pastor to our parish in River Forest, St. Luke's. So we became very close. Our move to California separated us, unfortunately, but he visited here occasionally, and we made frequent trips to Chicago for our families there.

Another priest made us feel proud of our work teaching skating at the skating school. A young Father Cox came to us and asked for private lessons during the day because he drove down from a small town in the middle of Wisconsin and had to drive back before evening. It turned out that he wanted to learn enough to teach skating to the children in his town as a means of keeping them interested in the church. He froze a natural ice rink on the church grounds to give free skating to the community. It was very popular with the town and became a focal point of interest. We became quite involved with him and brought skaters up there to put on ice shows for him and the townspeople. It was cold skating in the freezing northern wind, but it was gratifying to feel we were giving something back for all the good breaks we had with the skating school business.

The friendliest priest we have met in recent years is Father Jim Poulsen of St. Gregory, the Great parish in Scripps Ranch part of San Diego. It was luck that we bought our condo in his parish, and we soon realized how lucky we were. We had just taken over the San Diego Ice Arena, and as part of the opening festivities we asked Father Jim to bless the operation. When he arrived for the ceremony he picked up a pair of rental skates without our knowledge, so when he was introduced for the blessing he skated out across the ice much to our surprise. So Father Jim became our second skating priest. We have tried to keep in touch with him on our visits to Tom and Cyndi's in San Diego. We hope he can meet our other children who have had marriage differences with the Church, since he has a very enlightened view of how those differences can be resolved.

Probably the most famous priest we have met was Bishop Fulton Sheen of television fame. A neighbor of ours in River Forest was Pat Carey, a beautiful young girl in St. Luke's Parish who had been disabled by polio and was confined to a wheelchair. Somehow she had met Bishop Sheen, and they became good friends. The bishop would fly into Chicago once a week to do a television show for a local sponsor. This was before videotape, so he had to do the show live. Pat Carey frequently invited us to go to the airport to meet the bishop, so we got to know him very well. Once we went to New York with Pat and had meals at the bishop's house while we stayed in a hotel across the street.

Our family has been greatly enhanced by the in-laws and their families brought into it by the marriages of our children. Some we have become closer to than others, due to normal similar interests. We feel close to Cathy's husband Jimmy Tanner and his family since we had the wedding at their town in North Carolina, and since Norah became involved for a number of years in selling their Doncaster line of women's clothing—which is sold in the home. We have also enjoyed visiting at their beautiful summer home in South Carolina. On the day of Cathy's wedding I happened to be entering the club for the reception with Jimmy's mother, Ellyn Tanner. Many of our family had been in town for the week and having many festivities including the rehearsal dinner the night before. So Ellyn gave me a nice compliment when she said she always thought her family was too wild until she met mine!

We've enjoyed Cyndi's family since we had her wedding to Tom at our home in San Diego. We met most of her family then. We also visit Tom and Cyndi frequently, since they have our newest grandchildren, Christina and Jennifer, and meet Cyndi's family there. We consider them all to be additions to our list of friends as well as family.

Probably the group of friends with the greatest longevity has been those we have met through skating. We still enjoy getting together with those childhood friends we spent so many hours with at the skating clubs of our early days. Ralph McCreath, who recently passed away, Don Gilchrist, Marg and Bruce Hyland from the Toronto Skating Club days we still see often even though geography makes it difficult. It has been especially gratifying recently to talk to my "girlfriend" Mary Robinette, now Mrs. Burke Seitz, in Toronto. I had heard that they had married, so I called, and they told me they had been married ten years. But only after three they were able to marry in the Church, and they were very happy. Burke was a friend of mine in high school at St. Mike's, and I knew he would be a great husband for Mary. I'm sure they'll be very happy.

Speaking of geography, we are even still in touch with skaters from all over the world we have met through international competitions and ice shows, from Bobby Hirai in Tokyo, who arranged our meeting with the wealthy Japanese businessman; Reidar Borjeson in Oslo; in London and Amsterdam, Betty Goodheart, whose husband Skee, president of *Holiday on Ice* and a lifelong friend, died recently; also in London, Maxine and Alfonso dels Prats, who have parties for us when we're in town; and so many others that I have trouble listing them all. We still keep in touch with the Mandys in South Africa.

The other group of skating friends consists of those we have worked with in *Ice Follies*, most of whom we recently saw at the sixty-year reunion in Lake Arrowhead. We became close to a special Ice Folliette, Gail Foster Pitts, when she taught at the first Ice Capades Chalet at Topanga. Gail was instrumental in organizing and running the very successful reunion, and we are so pleased that we have been able to know her and her husband, Don. Friends from the *Ice Capades* shows and Chalets have also become very close and many are close neighbors here in the desert. These include Donna Atwood Harris of *Ice Capades* fame; Arnold Shoda; Bob Turk, former choreographer and producer of *Ice Capades*; and many others.

One very special friend whom we first met at the Westwood Sonja Henie Ice Palace and the *Sonja Henie Hollywood Ice Revue*, Susan Strong Davis, has become more than just a former skating friend. Although we lost touch for many years while we were living in Chicago and Newport Beach, a few years ago we got together again and have been very close ever since. Susan was one of the two girls I drove out to Los Angeles with in 1950 when Norah was expecting Ann. She was the one who couldn't drive the stick shift. So the other girl and I were the original "Driving Miss Davis." Susan has become a benefactor of many skaters who need financial help. Norah encouraged her to do so and helped select the skaters who needed help, because at that time Norah was the "goodwill ambassador," a euphemism for "talent scout," for *Ice Capades*, so she was in constant touch with all potentially good skaters from all over the country. Susan and Norah have become even closer friends by sharing this interest in skating and skaters. One of the first skaters Norah suggested to Susan became a national pair champion and Olympic and World bronze medalist and is now the coach of many champion skaters, Peter Oppergard, who is almost a son to Susan.

Norah visits most of the major international and national skating competitions with Susan and looks forward to them every year. Susan has become not only a good friend of ours but also an exceedingly good friend of a number of young skaters who need the help she so generously gives them.

Another couple we met through skating who became lifelong friends is Wina Richardson and her husband John. Norah met

Wina with Susan Strong while skating at the Westwood Ice Palace, and they became good friends. When the war was over and John returned from the Canadian Navy, we all hit it off well and spent much time together. John was a champion-level golfer and had won a scholarship in ice hockey to the University of Southern California. He played some professional hockey in Los Angeles, and I would take Norah and Wina to the games. Both girls were well along on their first pregnancies, and when got excited at the games—which they always did—and started jumping up and down and yelling at the referees, I was sure I'd be delivering a couple of babies right there in the stands. It was scary. John's golf was great and he was so patient with me (because mine wasn't), that he would try to help me. We went to Pebble Beach, one of the toughest courses in the country, a few times, and while he played it in par, I lost count of my strokes by the fifth hole.

A great wealth of friends of ours has come from our pupils in skating—from some of the little tiny tot classes to the world champions I had the pleasure of training when I was coach for principals with *Ice Capades* shows. Among the former, the one who has remained closest to us and whom we consider part of our immediate family, is Lynn Holly Johnson, now Mrs. Kelly Givens. Lynn Holly began as a tiny tot in our skating school in Park Ridge, Illinois, and went on to become a figure skating competitor and a skating partner with our son David. As pair skaters in their early years they even beat Tai Babalonia and Randy Gardner, who later won a world championship. Lynn was skating a specialty number in *Ice Capades* when I had a call from a Hollywood movie producer asking if we knew of any young girl skater of competitive level who knew anything about blindness. I was astounded because that fit the description of Lynn Holly perfectly. As a young girl she played the part of Helen Keller in the play *The Miracle Worker* in a Chicago production. The producer auditioned Lynn, and she got the lead part in the movie *Ice Castles*, in which she plays the part of a young skater who goes blind from a bad fall while skating.

Lynn Holly participated in another phase of our lives when we were active in sailboat racing in Southern California. She frequently served as one of our crew members on our thirty-six-foot Islander. On two- or three-day ocean races, she was our chief cook and a very good one. Those racing days were most satisfying, especially with the competitive attitude we had developed in skating. The competition was fierce on the water at the start of the race or rounding a buoy when everyone is jockeying for position; but it stopped at the water's edge when the camaraderie accelerated in the club after the races. This group was the source of many good friends. We started in Newport Harbor at Voyagers Yacht Club with the Grants, Marilyn and Les, but transferred to Bahia Corinthian when Hobie Denny, who was commodore of BCYC, became a partner in our boat, *Stroker*. We won a few races and usually trophied particularly when John Tatum came in as a partner and thought of the name Stroker. John was an excellent helmsman and could get the most out of the wind for the boat. The "Friday Lunch Bunch" grew from the boaters at BCYC, and it included some of the best friends of my later years. I miss all of them, especially those who have gone, such as Willie Williamson, Al Cassel, and Dick Menkin. Incidentally, in all my years as a member of yacht clubs, I never heard anyone refer to their boat as a yacht; it was always just a boat.

As a skating coach for *Ice Capades* I had the exciting job of training world champions, Otto and Maria Jelinek, Aja Zanova, and other great skaters. They were easy to work with because they were humble enough to realize that they still needed coaching. We became close friends with many of them and still see them occasionally. Dorothy Hamil is a neighbor here in the desert, and she and I just appeared on a *Biography* special on Sonja Henie.

But the quintessential friends who started as pupils are members of the Barrett family of Niles, Illinois. We spent many a pleasant vacation with them, including one in Kenora when they came up there with us. Our fondest and sometime funniest times with Tom and Carol were in our sailboat *Fine-A-Lee*, which we owned as partners. We never have fried chicken livers with mustard without thinking of them for introducing us to this delicacy.

Another group of friends who started as pupils and became close friends are many young ladies and men whom we taught in Chicago as teenagers: Gladys Jacobs, who became movie star Lara Lindsay, now Mrs. Howard Ladd; Dorothy Ann Nelson Fenno, who was Richard Dwyer's skating partner in *Ice Follies*; and many others who achieved recognition as performers or teachers. Janet Lynn, former National Figure Skating champion, began her career as Janet Novicki at our #2 Skating School on Loomis Boulevard on Chicago's south side. So many skaters started at one of our schools that today most of the skating instructors at the many rinks in the Chicago area were our pupils at one time.

A great family of friends developed when one of their daughters wanted to spend some time at Ice Capades Chalet in Costa Mesa where the world-famous coach John Nicks was teaching. Tamie Klindworth was a friend of David's from skating events, so we made arrangements for her to stay with us on Balboa Island for a year or so. It was very convenient for us since she drove and could take young David with her for the early morning "patch" session. We still see the Klindworths at skating events and have been trying to take them up on their invitation to spend some time on their sailboat in the Caribbean.

The song from *The King and I* contains the line, "By your pupils you'll be taught," and it is certainly true for us. We wish we could name all of our pupils who have contributed to our growth and happiness in our lives.

Although he did not become a friend in the usual sense, a man who taught me a great deal in one evening and whom I consider the "Most Unforgettable Man I Ever Met," is the Zulu Chief Mangosuthu Buthelezi. His wisdom about the true nature of the African tribes is still being carried out in most of sub-Saharan Africa, convincing me that his comparison to America in the sixteenth and seventeenth centuries has given me a greater understanding and sympathy for the civil misunderstandings that are going on all around us.

The year we celebrated our fiftieth wedding anniversary, 1994, also happened to be the fiftieth anniversary for movie star Charleton Heston and his wife. When he was interviewed and asked how they were able to keep a marriage for fifty years, especially in Hollywood, he replied, "By using three little words frequently." When the announcer said that he must mean, "I love you." Heston said, "No, three better words are, 'I was wrong!'" From our marriage experience which I consider to be the strength of this book and its main theme, I must agree with his wisdom.

An appropriate note on which to end this memorium must be Dorothy Stevens's depiction of Sonja's funeral, as it appears to epitomize the extroverted character of the life of Sonja Henie.

The funeral service was beautiful. It was in the crematorium, which is an A-shaped building with a high-pitched roof. The seats were facing a large glass window which looked out to a circular courtyard banked with flowers. Everything was filled with flowers. Below the window was the casket flanked by tall tapers with the minister behind it. Red carpet had been laid from the entrance to the seats the Royal Family would use. Everyone was asked to be there fifteen minutes early, so they would all be there when the Royal Family arrived. When the day dawned, it was very dull and gray, making the service seem more somber. We were in our seats and heard the bugles announcing the Royal Family. Drums rolled, and everyone faced them as they walked on the red carpet to their seats. A Lutheran minister began the service. The casket was a plain wooden box with no metal or ornament, it is just white wood. Just as the minister finished the service and stood down by the casket, the clouds opened up at the peak of the window and a bright beam of sunlight shone on the casket like a spotlight; it made the casket look like marble, a shining marble with a bank of red roses behind it. As the minister said the words "dust to dust," the clouds closed in again, and it was a dull gray day as we filed out. There was a huge crowd of people outside waiting to file past the casket, which was never opened. The spotlight of sun was a repeat of what was known as "Sonja Henie weather." When we played the show in Oslo in 1953, which was one of her greatest triumphs, we played Jordahl Amphi, which has a large opening in the roof so the ice area is exposed—although there is a roof over the seating area. It was in August, which is a rainy month there, and it rained heavily every day. We pulled canvas over the ice to protect it, but as showtime came the rain would stop and the moon would come out. As soon as the show was over the rain would begin again. The papers referred to it as "Sonja Henie weather!"

This story is dedicated to all the "good weather" Sonja brought to so many of us.